VAULT CAREER GUIDE TO THE FASHION INDUSTRY

VAULT CAREER GUIDE TO THE FASHION INDUSTRY

HOLLY HAN
AND THE STAFF OF VAULT

Library of Congress CIP Data is available.

ISBN 1-58131-201-6

Printed in the United States of America

ACKNOWLEDGEMENTS

Special thanks to my parents and Steve for supporting me in all my endeavors. I also wish to acknowledge those who let me interview them for this book - especially Sylvia and Karen who have been and suffered with me through much of my fashion career.

Thanks to everyone who had a hand in making this book possible, especially Marcy Lerner, Ed Shen, Jake Wallace and Kelly Shore. We are also extremely grateful to Vault's entire staff of writers, editors and interns for all their help in the editorial and production processes.

Vault also would like to acknowledge the support of Matt Doull, Ahmad Al-Khaled, Lee Black, Eric Ober, Hollinger Ventures, Tekbanc, New York City Investment Fund, Globix, Hoover's, Glenn Fischer, Mark Hernandez, Ravi Mhatre, Carter Weiss, Ken Cron, Ed Somekh, Isidore Mayrock, Zahi Khouri, Sana Sabbagh, and other Vault investors, as well as our family and friends.

Table of Contents

Visit Vault at **www.vault.com** for insider company profiles, expert advice,
career message boards, expert resume reviews, the Vault Job Board and more.

V/\ULT CAREER LIBRARY

ix

Visit Vault at **www.vault.com** for insider company profiles, expert advice,
career message boards, expert resume reviews, the Vault Job Board and more.

VAULT CAREER LIBRARY

xi

Introduction

Do you thrill to the thought that gray might – just might – be the new black? Do you tire of fashion trends before they even hit the stores? Then a career in fashion could be the right choice for you. Those who truly love the field say that the perks – fabulous clothes, exposure to famous people and brands, extraordinary diversity, awareness of upcoming trends and cool job status-are worth the struggle. Still, fashion is not all glitz and glamour. Even more than talent, an understanding of the industry is what lands the job.

Even though the fashion industry is difficult to break into, opportunities abound – creative jobs in design and marketing; retail sales and buying positions; corporate careers in finance, planning, and distribution. This guide covers where to begin and what options are available in the industry.

Yet whether you are seeking a place on the catwalk or in the haute couture clubhouse, the fashion business is just that – a business. Insiders from all over the fashion world say that their jobs are high on stress and low on pay. Moreover, insiders aver, people are often judged as much on looks as on performance.

With its rigorous hours, capricious culture and wobbly corporate ladder, the fashion industry certainly isn't for everybody. Yet for a dedicated minority, there is no more exciting and inspiring place. Lecturing at a forum hosted by the Fashion Group Foundation, designer Isaac Mizrahi characterized fashion this way: "I hope you all adore what you're doing. It's really got to be this obsession. You have to love cloth. You have to love chalk. You have to love pins. You do it because you love to do it, and can't stop doing it."

Visit Vault at **www.vault.com** for insider company profiles, expert advice, career message boards, expert resume reviews, the Vault Job Board and more.

VAULT CAREER LIBRARY

1

THE SCOOP

VAULT CAREER LIBRARY

Fashion Industry Basics

CHAPTER 2

Industry Overview

Challenges and opportunities

Between 1997 and 2000, the U.S. economy expanded rapidly and the fashion industry grew along with it. The period was characterized by low unemployment, low inflation and greater access to credit, all of which spurred consumer spending. In the United States, the womenswear market grew 6.7 percent between 1997 and 2001 to a value of $139.9 billion according to research firm EuroMonitor. (Womenswear is the largest segment of the apparel and fashion industry, which consists of womenswear, menswear, childrenswear, and footwear.)

Since 2000, however, consumer confidence and spending have fallen due to rising unemployment and a weakened U.S. and world economy. The fashion industry also faces challenges. Women, the biggest consumers of fashion, are spending less time and money on clothes shopping. The trend toward "business casual" has also negatively impacted the industry's sales as many consumers don't need separate pricey outfits for their professional lives. Consumers have also become used to low prices due to the discount practices of major retailers such as Target and Kohl's. Value-conscious consumers, trained by frequent sales to expect bargains, wait for clothing to go on sale before purchasing.

However, certain areas of the fashion industry are growing. For example, the plus-size segment of the womenswear market, little more than a niche opportunity in the 1990s, has grown into an established category for the women's apparel industry. (We'll examine emerging trends in greater depth later in this chapter in the Industry Trends section.)

Overall, the clothing & footwear market is highly fragmented, with the top five manufacturers accounting for only 11.8 percent of industry value sales in 1998. The five leading companies in the U.S. clothing and footwear market are Sara Lee Inc, VF Corporation, Levi Strauss Co., Liz Claiborne Inc. and Fruit of the Loom Inc. Private label products, also called store brands, were estimated to account for approximately 24 percent of total market value in 1998.

Visit Vault at **www.vault.com** for insider company profiles, expert advice, career message boards, expert resume reviews, the Vault Job Board and more.

V∧ULT CAREER LIBRARY   5

Fashion and tech

Although fashion companies are adept at predicting shades of color that will be popular two years in advance, insiders say that fashion manufacturers often lag behind the rest of the corporate world when it comes to technology. Insiders agree that apparel manufacturing runs far more efficiently with the latest technological advancements. Still, many small firms have not yet made the capital investment in computerized cutters, sewing machines and other production devices. Most small firms can't afford to or don't believe it's necessary. Many larger firms, on the other hand, are connected to their retail distributors though the latest and most powerful computer networks. According to Joseph Morgan, founder of Jaral Fashion Personnel in 1966, the industry has changed in the following ways: First, if you want to be a designer, you must be able to design on a computer (Macs are most popular); it's not possible to rely only on pencil and paper. Second, the industry is much more global because almost everything sold domestically is produced overseas.

In addition, the retail space for fashion has changed. Apparel is one of the biggest retail categories on the Internet, with U.S. sales of about $5.2 billion in 2002, up from $4.4 billion in 2001, according to Shop.org, the online arm of the National Retail Federation. Gap Inc., the largest U.S. specialty apparel retailer (with sales of over $13 billion last year), has added retail sales from the Internet to combat the recent decline in earnings. The company introduced gap.com in 1997, later following with web sites for its Banana Republic and Old Navy brands. Gap uses its Internet presence not only to sell clothing available in its stores but also to stock merchandise not available in stores, such as maternity clothing and Banana Republic petite sizes.

A worldwide industry

Fashion has always been a worldwide industry. The names of fashion's global hotspots roll easily off the tongue: New York, London, Tokyo, Milan and Paris. It's all interconnected. In fact, insiders claim that the U.S. forecasts its fashion trends based on what Europe is already doing. Explains one American fashion forecaster: "Europe is always one season ahead of the U.S. To get a look at the future of fashion, my company will actually send people to Paris. There, they'll check out what people are wearing, what new styles are in the windows. They examine new colors, designs and accessories; and then they report back." Asia – particularly Japan – is another up-and-comer. "Like Europe, Asia also influences the future of fashion in the United States," reports another source.

Despite Europe's fashion prowess, the region is not immune to the industry's ups and downs. In the late 1990s, for example, apparel and textile sectors floundered. According to a 1997 survey, some 60,000 to 150,000 textile and apparel jobs are lost annually throughout Europe. Western Europe may be the world's trendsetter, but apparel and textile jobs in France and Italy are quickly disappearing to lower-wage workers in other countries. Germany is apparently suffering its worst job losses within the industry since the end of World War II. Among European competitors, Great Britain is one of the few success stories, showing growth in the textile and apparel markets.

Outsourcing overseas

Due to cheaper labor costs overseas, U.S. fashion companies outsource much of their production work. In many Asian countries, where labor laws are lax or even nonexistent, garment contractors force workers to accept long hours in hazardous conditions. In a place like Indonesia, pay is only pennies a week. Many of these workers are under the age of 14. Apparel manufacturers have started reevaluating their production due to an intensified focus on sweatshops and unfair labor conditions across the world. Among the apparel-producing countries, cites one 1996 survey, wages vary to a staggering degree, with the U.S. average at $9.56/hour, Germany's at $23.19/hour, and Bangladesh's at 10 cents/hour. Meanwhile, as the U.S. Department of Labor gets tougher on wage violators, disgruntled and desperate U.S. manufacturers are going overseas for the cheapest available workforce.

In addition, the domestic market for apparel and textile manufacturing is shrinking. According to the U.S. Department of Labor, there are approximately 530,000 people employed in the apparel industry in 2002, compared to 1,007,200 in 1992. The top apparel employers by state are California, New York and Texas. New York City, the number one city for fashion industry employment, which includes textile as well as apparel manufacturing, and apparel wholesaling, has seen employment drop 6.3 percent from 1999 and 25.6 percent since 1991. Almost all U.S. apparel companies design domestically but source goods internationally to take advantage of free trade agreements with low-wage countries. The U.S. manufacturers that have survived tend to offer quick turnaround for design and production.

Visit Vault at **www.vault.com** for insider company profiles, expert advice, career message boards, expert resume reviews, the Vault Job Board and more.

VAULT CAREER LIBRARY   7

While the situation is far from optimal, the loss in U.S. production jobs is somewhat offset by a surge in international opportunities. To manage their importing and exporting, U.S.-based companies with international production plants must employ supervisors, managers and coordinators. Hence, fashion professionals who are fluent in foreign languages or willing to work overseas can find great opportunities. And production isn't the only option. Those interested in trend services and design may also find overseas jobs.

Paying attention to the market

Many professionals working in the fashion industry draw their inspiration from the lives of famous designers. Names like Armani and Versace are not only synonymous with gorgeous upscale apparel, but also with glamorous images and lifestyles. Fashion amateurs sometimes picture themselves designing apparel for a wealthy clientele, launching new collections to applause and rose bouquets and schmoozing with supermodels and celebrities. A professional at the Parsons School of Design in New York City confirms this common focus on high fashion: "People who love fashion and who are creative want to do bridge, couture or evening wear. They are not thinking about the market."

The reality, however, is that few people in the fashion industry achieve fame and fortune. With this in mind, realistic fashion professionals are opting for more secure (if slightly less sexy) jobs. Successful companies such as Polo, Tommy Hilfiger and The Gap manage specific – but not narrow – markets. Aside from talent and good marketing, these companies owe their success to close tracking of cultural trends. "While many designers would love to design elegant business attire, corporate America has embraced casual wear and 'dress down' suits," reports a fashion insider in production. "Activewear and sportswear are 'in.' Companies like Abercombie and Fitch have made a bundle acting on consumer trends."

Mega-brands

These days, retailers are focused on creating "mega-brands." Ed Razek, Limited's president and chief marketing officer, has been quoted as saying, "Building brands is like making movies." Even huge brands like Levi's must believe this to be true. Levi's is designing, producing and marketing an increasing number of styles at different prices, sold through a range of retailers. The apparel manufacturer wants to reach every customer by purposely segmenting the brand. After years of selling to department stores like Macy's and Foley's and avoiding mass merchants, Levi's announced plans for summer 2003 to create a new brand for Wal-Mart stores called "Levi Strauss Signature" that will sell for below $30. At the other end of the spectrum, Levi's also sells "Levi Strauss Vintage" to exclusive retailers like Neiman Marcus and Barneys New York for $85 to $220. These styles features unique finishes and vintage designs from Levi's archives.

In the cosmetics industry, Revlon is betting on a new line of berry and frost-colored lipsticks, blushes and eye shadows promoted by Halle Berry, a Revlon "spokesmodel" and co-star of the 2002 James Bond film *Die Another Day*. It is one of the largest new product promotions in years for Revlon. The company hopes that the Bond-themed products will triple retail shipments for the last quarter of 2002 as compared to last year. Revlon hopes that the co-branding effort will generate the sales that Revlon needs to reverse four years of losses.

The Hierarchy

Not all apparel is alike. Fashion professionals generally use these categories to identify different markets:

Haute couture

Haute couture is often considered the pinnacle of designer clothing. Its origins can be traced to Paris more than 150 years ago. Haute couture involves craftsmanship, the skill of the dressmakers and embellishers (feather makers, embroiderers, milliners) who create the finery of the exceptional. It is tailored and carefully produced for each client. Although couture apparel is seen almost exclusively on the supremely wealthy or on the runway, designers of haute couture influence all levels of the fashion industry. There are only eighteen houses of haute couture in France today since requirements are stringent: Balmain, Pierre Cardin, Carven, Chanel, Christian Dior, Louis Féraud, Givenchy, Lecoanet Henant, Christian Lacroix, Lapidus, Guy Laroche, Hanae Mori, Paco Rabanne, Nina Ricci, Yves Saint Laurent, Jean-Louis Scherrer, Torrente, and Emanuel Ungaro. Prices range from $16,000 to $20,000 for a woman's tailored suit to $60,000 and up for an evening gown.

Designer (or Prêt à porter)

Designer is the step down from couture. Prêt à porter can be translated as "ready to wear." While not as exorbitantly priced as couture, designer

Visit Vault at **www.vault.com** for insider company profiles, expert advice, career message boards, expert resume reviews, the Vault Job Board and more.

VAULT CAREER LIBRARY

9

apparel is nevertheless still expensive. Designer clothing is sold in specialty stores, department stores and boutiques – almost everywhere. Some prominent designers are Anna Sui, Chloé, Dolce & Gabbana, Giorgio Armani, Hugo Boss and Junya Watanabe.

Bridgewear

Bridge is the step down from designer fashions. This apparel is generally much more affordable and available at better department stores. Although several steps down from fashion's pinnacle, bridgewear is nevertheless considered more exclusive than "better" clothing. Top designers such as Donna Karan and Calvin Klein knock themselves off to produce very popular bridgewear lines such as DKNY and CK.

Better

Nationally recognized brand names, such as Liz Claiborne, Ann Taylor, or Nordstrom's private label. Customers usually expect a particular image, quality, or price point from a better brand.

Moderate

Moderate describes many nationally known sportswear brands or lower priced "better" national brands. Examples of moderate brands include Dockers, Limited and The Gap.

Budget

Budget falls into the least expensive category. Many brands include private labels for discount merchants, such as Jaclyn Smith or Kathy Ireland (for K-Mart house brands). Old Navy is one of the most prominent budget brands.

Emerging Trends

Even in a cold market, there are hot spots. Currently sizzling markets include private label, women's plus size clothing, customized clothing and technology accessories.

Tech garb

Manufacturers are merging technology with apparel to create new products for the market. Wrinkle-free or "no-iron" shirts came out decades ago, but they still required occasional ironing. In the early 1990s, wrinkle-free shirts were improved by adding a wrinkle-resistant coating. The newest generation of wrinkle-free shirts is patented by TAL Corp. of Hong Kong. The process involves baking a special coating onto the fabric as well as an innovative use of adhesives along the seams to prevent pockets, cuffs and plackets from puckering. Modifications to the coating formula allow designers to use broadcloth (a soft flat weave) rather than the heavier cotton-shirting fabrics used in wrinkle-free dress shirts previously. Retailers that carry the TAL wrinkle-free shirts include Nordstrom, Men's Wearhouse, Brooks Brothers and Jos. A. Bank Clothiers. Other fabrics, usually made with Teflon, resist stains as well.

Technology fashion accessories are also becoming increasingly popular. These accessories range from stylish carrying cases for laptops to fashionable cell phone covers. In the future, cell phones, personal digital assistants and miniature computers may be integrated into wearable devices. Manufacturers are using more technology in the production of clothing as well. It allows the retailer to offer a unique product to each customer. According to Michael Hong, (see profile in the Design and Product Development chapter) Director of Product Development of Outwear at Kenneth Cole, "I'm always looking for something new. Technology is always moving. I want to infuse technology into life. So I choose clothes as the medium because we all wear it."

Private label

Private label clothing, footwear and accessories are products that are designed for a particular retailer. The advantages of private label for retailers are many: flexibility in pricing, control over product, cost and advertising, exclusivity, in-house design and, most importantly, a bigger share of the profit margin. (Of course, one disadvantage is that retailers must eat the costs of any unpopular products.) It is common for retailers, department stores and

Visit Vault at **www.vault.com** for insider company profiles, expert advice, career message boards, expert resume reviews, the Vault Job Board and more.

VAULT CAREER LIBRARY **11**

mail order catalogs to launch their own private label. In the mid-1990s, Federated (the parent of Macy's and other department stores) increased its overall private brands program and established a strong market for exclusive private label products such as I·N·C/International Concepts, Alfani, Charter Club and Tools of the Trade. Although there are no official numbers on retailer-owned brand market share, best estimates are that 15 to 25 percent of the goods in major stores are private label.

Advantages to the retailer:

• Reduce manufacturer dominance in the store

• Create more dependence on the retailer by the consumer

• Become closer to the customer

• Retail buyers understand products better

• Build brand image for the retailer and provide product variety

• More freedom in pricing strategy and increased gross margins

Disadvantages for the retailer:

• Backlash from manufacturers, who may receive smaller orders from the retailer or perceive the private label as direct competitor

• Increased financial responsibilities and lack of financial support from suppliers

• The potential for excessive focus on the private label at the expense of other products

• Dissatisfaction with the private label product may cause consumers to stop shopping for other products at the retail outlets

Plus-size growth

Women's plus-size clothing, in sizes 14 to 28, is a growing niche market. Tired of the dowdy and uncomfortable styles marketed to plus-size consumers in the past, consumers are jumping to purchase new fashionable styles in larger sizes. Total retail sales for plus-size items in the year 2000 reached almost $32 billion, or 30 percent of the women's clothing market. More clothing manufacturers have created attractive, fashion-conscious options for larger women. The plus-size market has proven to be very brand loyal with increasing sales compared to other market segments.

Personalization

Tailored clothing used to be a pricey luxury reserved for the wealthy. Today, retailers such as Lands' End use body scanning to help customers order custom-fitted jeans and activewear for under $100. Even more traditional retailers like Brooks Brothers are betting that the technology will help more customers buy custom-fitted suits. It's a pretty simple and short experience for the customer. The customer steps into a measuring booth and a body scanning software program scans the person's body for about 12 seconds with a strobe light. A three-dimensional map is created from the scan that captures over 200,000 data points – everything from the circumference of wrists and biceps, to the chest, neck and shoulders. Customers can then purchase a custom fit suit, tuxedo, sport coat, blazer, trousers, or shirt.

Nike has launched an online personalized service allowing shoppers to pick the colors they want on their running shoes or cross trainers. The service, named NikeID, also allows customers to choose a name or nickname, up to eight letters, stitched on the shoe. The initiative is a step toward broader customization of athletic shoes at Nike.

Our Survey Says: Fashion Industry Culture

Image

In the fashion industry, your image is an important factor in your career. In some fields, such as modeling, a certain "type" is required. In other fields, such as public relations, good looks are preferred. Evidence of fashion's obsession with appearance is everywhere. Many retail employees must sport the clothing of their company. Designers serve as walking examples of their work. Even employees at fashion magazines "dress accordingly." Appearance is more important for fashion professionals who interact with the public and who work for high-end employers. (If you work in finance or planning, your dress matters less. And if you work at Kohl's versus Bloomingdale's, being "fashionable" is not as important.)

The "beauty prerequisite" is a source of pride, but also of contention. "You're often judged by what you wear and what you look like," says a designer who specializes in women's couture. Noverto Gonzalez, who worked as an assistant buyer at Saks Fifth Avenue says, "You have to represent whom you work for. The industry can be pretentious. They look at your shoes, bag and

Visit Vault at www.vault.com for insider company profiles, expert advice, career message boards, expert resume reviews, the Vault Job Board and more.

VAULT CAREER LIBRARY   13

watch to check out the label." Certainly, appearance alone probably won't make or break a fashion career. Most fashion employers are looking for traditional skills and abilities. Nevertheless, in the fashion industry appearance may count more than it does in other industries.

Read the magazines and follow celebrities if you want to keep up with the latest trends. Check the publication section in this guide for trade papers, but also consider magazine staples like *Vogue, Harper's Bazaar* and *W*. You may also want to look at the French, English or Spanish editions of these magazines.

Do good and be beautiful

Fashion is home to glamour, beautiful people and of course, celebrities. Everyone knows the name of at least one supermodel; most people could name quite a few more. In fashion, namedropping and networking are the norm. But another common, if less known, aspect of the fashion world is philanthropy. "Philanthropy," designer Kenneth Cole said at a fashion charity event, "has been part of our corporate culture from the beginning."

This warm-and-fuzzy consciousness isn't simply motivated by the heart: the wallet has something to do with it. Specifically, mixing philanthropy with commerce is a sales tool called cause-related marketing. Since public service is an ideal conduit for sales, many famous designers embrace one cause or another. However, these causes are often as changeable as the industry itself. Points out one fashion insider: "Fashion may embrace fur-wearing one day and protest it the next. Its loyalties are superficial." There are drawbacks to here-today-gone-tomorrow activism. Nevertheless, public service organizations can benefit by the media attention given to "fashionable causes."

Melting pot

The glass ceiling is not much of a problem in an industry where "women outnumber men." "Race is rarely, if ever, an issue" and "a large number of the men in design are gay," says an insider at an upscale department store. In fact, an insider at The Gap is happy to report, "Gender and ethnicity are just not an issue." In almost all aspects of the industry, the pervasion of different cultures, races, religious faiths and sexual orientations is common. "I expected to see a lot of white upper-class yuppies," remarks one J. Crew insider, "but this wasn't what I envisioned. The proverbial New York City melting pot boils over into the [J. Crew] corporate office."

L'Oreal is one brand that prides itself on its international flavor. In fact, it boasts that many of its employees are multilingual. Nike is also sound in the diversity department. At this company, different ethnic groups gather for "informal meetings." One member of the company's "Hispanic caucus" finds Nike "a fun place to meet other Latinos and network." Of course, not all employees are content with their company's heterogeneity. At companies like Lands End and L.L. Bean, some employees complain of a lack of diversity. But others argue that the predominately white demographics simply reflect the surrounding communities. "Maine and Wisconsin are not exactly known for large mixes of ethnic communities," says one. "It would follow that the minority headcount is proportional to the community and state." An Asian-American L.L. Bean insider agrees, "I have always felt that the employee makeup simply reflects the general population [in Maine]." As production continues to grow overseas, fashion industry employees are becoming more accustomed to a global marketplace. Companies may buy their fabric from Korea, cut and sew in Sri Lanka, pack and ship in Hong Kong, warehouse in the U.S. and sell in Canada and Mexico.

While the fashion industry is one of the most ethnically diverse around, insiders still complain of "a herd mentality." Complains one: "At my last job, everyone had a blonde bob. Fortunately, my new job is more diverse. It doesn't seem that race or sexuality is that important – it's all about how you look. Class and style are what are most important." Speaking of blondes, one celebrity dresser "can't wait to dress Gwyneth Paltrow." Why? "Because everyone wants to dress her!" He continues, "I enjoy meeting celebrities on a personal level, although not everything about my job is glamorous. It's not glamorous running around buying shoes at the last minute and sitting around a seating chart at 3 a.m., guessing who will be happy sitting next to each other." An assistant designer agrees that the industry is, at best, unpredictable. "I'm not doing what I thought I'd be doing," she says. "There are some people [in this industry] with high profile jobs, but most of us end up working for other famous people."

Visit Vault at **www.vault.com** for insider company profiles, expert advice,
career message boards, expert resume reviews, the Vault Job Board and more.

VAULT CAREER LIBRARY   15

VAULT CAREER GUIDES
GET THE INSIDE SCOOP ON TOP JOBS

"Cliffs Notes for Careers"
– FORBES MAGAZINE

Vault guides and employer profiles have been published since 1997 and are the premier source of insider information on careers.

Each year, Vault surveys and interviews thousands of employees to give readers the inside scoop on industries and specific employers to help them get the jobs they want.

"To get the un-varnished scoop, check out Vault"
– SMARTMONEY MAGAZINE

Education

Prestigious fashion schools like the Fashion Institute of Technology still thrive, but the industry has broadened its career reach. Fashion strongholds across the world – from major department stores to specialized, upscale boutiques – are now on the lookout for qualified candidates from all backgrounds. Companies are scouring colleges and universities, design programs and business schools for positions in retail, finance, buying or merchandising.

New York, New York

Rumor has it that New York City is the only place for fashion. And while New York is inarguably a fashion bastion, not all is ripe and juicy in the Big Apple. Fashion openings are not only extremely competitive in NYC; they are also low-paying. Sometimes, a fashion career counselor confesses, it is better to start your career elsewhere. "NYC may be the fashion capital of the world, but the truth is, companies outside of the city pay more because they need new talent. Besides, if you work with a large company, you can always relocate."

New York is probably the best city in the United States to study the industry because it's home to the biggest concentration of fashion companies. (Design and fashion degrees are often important for design jobs, as well as for potential entrepreneurs.) The city's three leading fashion schools are the Parsons School of Design, the Fashion Institute of Technology, and the Pratt Institute (located in Brooklyn). These schools funnel graduates into entry-level positions at the top design studios/houses. Each school has a year-end fashion show, which is always well attended by industry insiders looking for fresh talent. And New York City isn't the only New York educational option. "I earned my degree at Syracuse in upstate New York," says an assistant designer. "And I can't think of a better school."

A career counselor at a major school declares, "New York companies recruit predominately from New York schools and other New York companies." This is good news for New York fashion grads, although the pay scale isn't quite as pleasing. Fashion school graduates who opt to stay in New York can expect to make between $20,000 and $30,000 in entry-level design and retail jobs. Fashion associates, or those with two-year degrees, tend to earn less. Fortunately, in fashion, work experience soon becomes more important than educational background.

Visit Vault at **www.vault.com** for insider company profiles, expert advice, career message boards, expert resume reviews, the Vault Job Board and more.

VAULT CAREER LIBRARY   **17**

Outside the Big Apple

The West Coast is also home to top fashion schools, most notably the Fashion Institute of Design and Merchandising and Otis College of Art and Design in Los Angeles. There are also excellent design programs at many colleges and universities on both coasts – and in between. Check the appendix for a listing of schools.

If you're looking for a career change into fashion, a graduate program may be a wise choice. Many of these schools also have graduate programs. Go to http://www.gradschools.com/listings/menus/design_craft_menu.html to see a listing of graduate schools and their programs. Unfortunately, there are few continuing education classes for those already established in the industry. Most people go to trade shows or seminars thrown by industry groups to keep up with new trends, innovations and developments.

Decide what area of the fashion industry interests you most, as that will determine the type of school you should attend. If you prefer to do something on the business side, you may not need to attend a fashion school. You just need to get a solid background in business, accounting or economics. On the other hand, if you want to pursue a career in design, attending a fashion school will be a big plus.

Major Fashion Programs

The Fashion Institute of Technology

The Fashion Institute of Technology, or FIT for short (fitnyc.suny.edu), is a great choice for future fashion industry professionals. Its status as a New York state university makes it more affordable to the aspiring fashion virtuoso. FIT offers a wide variety of online offerings, including courses through the State University of New York Learning Network. The program includes courses in advertising and marketing communications, fashion design, and manufacturing management. Alumni include David Chu, founder of Nautica, and Andrea Jovine.

Otis College of Art and Design

Located in Los Angeles, Otis graduates work at Mattel, Guess, Puma, Levi Strauss, Wet Seal, BCBG and Abercrombie & Fitch. Todd Oldham, founder of Todd Oldham Jeans, says, "When I am asked what design school I would recommend, I always and wholeheartedly recommend Otis. Otis nurtures creativity in the most appealing ways: through support, encouragement, kindness and knowledge. Certainly the recipe for success. Otis rules!"

Parsons School of Design

Parsons School of Design (parsons.edu), founded in 1896, is a division of the New School University. The curriculum includes fashion as well as architectural design, fine arts, graphic design, interior design, photography, product design, and many others. The alumni list includes Donna Karan, Isaac Mizrahi, Anna Sui, Steven Meisel and Norman Rockwell.

Philadelphia University, School of Textiles

Philadelphia offers undergraduate and graduate programs in textile design, textile technology, textile engineering, and textile materials science. Firms such as Liz Claiborne, Nike, Burlington, Milliken and DuPont provide co-op and internship opportunities to students and recruit graduates.

Pratt Institute

Pratt Institute, usually called Pratt (pratt.edu), founded in 1887 and based in New York City, is known for a cross-disciplinary approach. Pratt is primarily an art school; only a small percentage of Pratt's student body study fashion. All students in the fashion department work as interns by senior year, many staying on at the same companies when they graduate. The school says, "The personal scale and exclusivity of the department play an important role in the success of its graduates." Pratt students get one-on-one attention from faculty and visiting professionals, such as Byron Lars and Mary McFadden.

Visit Vault at **www.vault.com** for insider company profiles, expert advice, career message boards, expert resume reviews, the Vault Job Board and more.

VAULT CAREER LIBRARY   **19**

Publications

There are a few vital information sources for the fashion industry. *Women's Wear Daily* (wwd.com) is a daily trade paper published by Fairchild Publications that covers international news regarding the fashion, beauty and retail industries. WWD is considered "the fashion bible" of the industry. On the West Coast, the fashion industry relies on *The Apparel News* (apparelnews.com), which covers the apparel and textile industries in California and the West Coast. Bobbin.com (a.k.a. "The Apparel Industry Magazine") describes itself as the business and technology authority for the sewn products industry.

Fairchild publications are also responsible for *DNR* and *FN*. *DNR* (dnrnews.com) is a weekly news magazine of men's fashion and retail. It provides news, in-depth features and market reports on men's wear retailing, design trends, apparel and textiles. *FN* or *Footwear News* (footwearnews.com) is a weekly publication for the international footwear community. For general fashion news, read *The New York Times'* "Fashion & Style" section. Mainstream magazines like *Vogue*, *Elle* and *Harper's Bazaar* are also must reads.

Getting Hired

CHAPTER 4

Networking

Ask around the fashion industry and you'll find people who dreamed of working there all their lives and people who stumbled into their positions by chance. One associate designer maintains, "To get into the creative end of the industry, you need a proper education. You need to study design. Technical people such as buyers and inventory planners, on the other hand, are more likely to have 'fallen' into their jobs." No matter how they got there, however, fashion professionals admit that having industry contacts is often more important than having talent. "To find a job," reveals an employee from Federated, "it's important to use the people you know. I found my first job through contacts, the next by sending an exploratory note and the third was luck – I got it out of a newspaper advertisement. I'd say my first job was the easiest to find."

While many people – and fashion students in particular – might feel dismayed by this need to know the "right people," one insider says worry is unnecessary. "Students often think they cannot make connections while confined within college walls," says a career counselor from a top New York fashion school. "This is a myth. Connections is just another word for relationships. You have relationships with other students, professors, career counselors, the school administration and many others. At fashion schools, most of the teachers have previous experience in the fashion industry." What does that mean? An acquaintance at your school or workplace might already have valuable job information!

It all comes down to networking. To find the right fashion job for you, it is necessary to discuss your job search with the people you know – and with the people they know. Ask questions, inquire about openings, and request informational interviews. Fashion students should attend as many college-sponsored events as possible and seek relevant internships. After a fashion internship has ended, they should keep in touch with their managers. A fashion career counselor confirms, "Those who serve as intern advisors often grow very fond of their interns. They want to know that you've graduated; they want to help and advise you."

Internships

Most fashion internships are in design, marketing, and production – and unpaid. Like the entertainment industry, actual education isn't as important as work experience. You will need some education to get in the door, but after that your resume or connections will get you farther. If you want to go into fashion or retail, get an internship or even a part-time job in sales or merchandising to get started. Each experience on your resume will help land a better internship or full-time job the next time. Although some internships are posted in the trade papers (check the Publications section), many internship searches are self-directed because many are never publicized. If the position is at a popular company or designer, the internship will never be posted since everyone will want it on his or her resume.

Make sure to express your desire to learn and help the company – even if you think your level of responsibility is not as high as you would like. Once you are in the company, you can find out about other positions before they may even be open. Build your resume, and you can get the interviews and introductions. Of course, your initial job in the fashion industry may not pay well. There are several options here – you work to get the experience or to learn enough to start your own business. If you are thinking of the latter, take any experience you can. It will pay off later.

Take initiative

While different fashion positions require different skills, most insiders agree that the industry overall calls for "initiative, patience and a strong degree of independence." One insider adds, "It's also great to have a boss who is going to be a good mentor and who will push you." Despite the glamour, prestige and job satisfaction, insiders have their gripes. "It's too competitive – both within the office and within the industry as a whole," says one informant. "People are sometimes unethical. For example, they might give you a commitment, but then drop the ball. Sometimes, clients cancel orders and I end up losing thousands of dollars – in one day." Fashion insiders toil long, strenuous hours. "It's a huge time commitment," offers another contact in buying. "I often start early and stay late – and I also travel a good part of the time. You lose perspective after so many hours." A different buyer adds, " I often spend 12 hours at work and eat lunch at my desk. Burnout. There's a lot of burnout."

Getting the job, acing the interview

There are two schools of thought in regard to moving up the fashion ranks. Some insiders swear that it's necessary to switch companies in order to climb. According to one knowing source, "Many companies have non-mobile positions, where employees are "pegged" in certain roles. In other words, if you're an assistant, everyone will always perceive you as an assistant." Others contend that it's best to stay put. "To move up the ranks, you have to be a hard worker, know the right people or lie on your resume," says one informant. "I was a hard worker. And I had a great boss who served as my mentor. By staying right where I was, I ended up moving up into key roles."

Once a job interview has been arranged, candidates should do extensive research on the company. Examine company literature and read the company web site. Browse through a periodical guide for the most recent articles on company developments. "Go to the library of a fashion school," advises another insider. "Ask someone to help you if you don't know how to find your information. In order for you to carry on a dialogue with the employer, you must know exactly how they work and what they do." Last, and perhaps most importantly, go shop the brand or retailer. You should know what type of products the company currently sells and carries. Also research the company's biggest competitors. General knowledge of key fashion players is also important. Insiders recommend brushing up on your mental database of trendsetters: Prada, Tommy Hilfiger, Calvin Klein, Donna Karan, Alexander McQueen and Ralph Lauren, among others.

On the big day, establish a rapport with the person who is interviewing you. "You can't be a bump on a log answering questions, even if you have a great resume and portfolio. Let your personality show through, because the interview is also about fit. Also," she continues, "don't ask about salary – at least, not on the first round." Ask intelligent questions about the company, position and even the interviewer's experience. Even if you lack experience in a particular area, an employer may hire you if he or she thinks you are quick and willing to learn.

As for dress code, insiders recommend careful consideration. Employers will certainly notice what interviewees wear and how they wear it. "As soon as they catch a glimpse of you, they make their decision," admonishes one theatrical designer. And while this scenario might not always hold true, it is a good idea to dress well. "Nothing radical," says another insider. "Unless you're a designer and they're looking for strange and futuristic looks." Another good tip: It's generally better to be slightly overdressed than underdressed.

ON THE JOB

Design and Product Development

CHAPTER 5

Designers create and produce garments, textiles and accessories. Some have formal training and some do not. Almost all designers begin as assistant designers for a few years and eventually become designers. In a large company, a designer may move up the ladder to be a design director. A design director manages the designers from each group. For example, at a company like Bebe, there may be a designer for each group (such as dresses, suits, knits, and denim), but a design director will coordinate the efforts of all the designers so the brand presents a cohesive image. Product development usually refers to retailers that develop their own product in conjunction with manufacturers. Product development differs from design in that it usually doesn't require as many technical skills. In fact, product developers may work with designers from other companies to create products for their own brand.

Jobs

Assistant Designer: Helps the designer create new designs. May help with sketches and research.

Designer: Creates plans for clothes that fit the image, season and price point of the brand.

Assistant Technical Designer: Assists designer or technical designer in all aspects of quality and fit procedures. Must have strong computer skills.

Technical Designer: Follows design direction to develop garments through technical sketches, specific measurements for garments, receiving and reviewing samples and sketching and measuring garments for technical packages.

Sample Pattern Maker: Translates designers' sketches into wearable works of art by draping and making patterns to create sample garments. Almost all patternmakers draft patterns on computers.

Textile Designer: Creates textiles by using various fibers and knitting or weaving techniques for industries ranging from apparel to upholstery.

Visit Vault at **www.vault.com** for insider company profiles, expert advice, career message boards, expert resume reviews, the Vault Job Board and more.

VAULT CAREER LIBRARY   **27**

The Scoop

Most fashion experts would agree that design, one of fashion's most competitive and exciting fields, requires technical and art training, leadership, ingenuity, highly developed patternmaking skills and a keen understanding of the aesthetic as well as the practical and cost-effective. Design also calls for absolute dedication. Some of the most successful designers refer to their vocation as an "obsession" or a "way of life." Given the hardships, designers have to be crazy about what they do. How else would they be able to survive the grueling hours, low entry-level pay, and lack of guarantees of success?

The first step toward becoming a designer is reconsidering your decision. Our insiders say there is no shame in being a realist: "Fashion students often come in bright-eyed and idealistic. They think they are ready for the hard work and difficult hours so long as they can have the glamour too. What they don't realize is that very, very few designers hit it big." Aspiring designers also err when it comes to focus. "You have to think about what consumers really want," advises another source. "It's vital to know the realities of the job market. Pay attention to what people are going to buy rather than what you want to create." And it never hurts to look at your other options. "Students don't know that there are a hundred other jobs in fashion besides design," says an insider from a New York fashion school. "There are trim buyers, pattern makers, sample makers, quality control experts and fashion consultants. Often, these jobs are not only better-paying, they are 100 percent more secure."

For those who have listened to the naysayers and still want to be designers, the advice is – go for it. Insiders from such famous New York City fashion schools as Pratt, Parsons and FIT all concede that someone has to be the next Donna Karan or Calvin Klein. Why not you? If you think you have the guts, the talent and the backbone, "go global and go for the top," declares one enthusiastic source.

The climb may take some time, however. "It's very rare for a young fashion designer to set up his own label immediately after graduation," confesses a source. In reality, most graduates will spend five or more years working for a designer, gaining experience, earning a reputation and making contacts. Some fashion professionals will even start a design career outside of the industry in order to break into the field. Internships at major fashion houses or other jobs, like pattern work or retail, can sometimes launch you into design. The bottom line: don't be too hasty. Think about each job as a stepping stone in your career – so that you will always know what options you have.

Getting Hired

Although fashion companies vary, almost all potential employers want to see a designer's portfolio before a hiring decision can be made. A portfolio typically contains four or five collections, each of which tells a story and a concept. A collection contains between eight and 15 drawings. Typically, it demonstrates basic art design skills as well as flat sketches and full-figure fashion illustrations. The stronger and more dynamic the portfolio, the better your chances of employment. Says a design source: "The portfolio is the main selling tool for a fashion design graduate. It needs to be current, fashion-forward and a reflection of the designer's sensibility and knowledge of the industry." She adds, "The portfolio should also be directed toward the company you're applying to." In others words, applicants should not submit bridge drawings to a company that specializes in casual clothing. On many interviews, employers will check a prospective designer's sketching abilities, use of color and technical work. They may also ask for additional flat sketches, technical sketches or specs.

Design jobs are attained through many means: industry connections or contacts, headhunters, internships and fashion publications. One associate designer who found her job through a headhunter asserts, "You have to push to get what you're looking for. The designer I worked with had faith in my skills, but the company wanted to hire someone with more experience. It's a matter of dealing with the powers that be, not the powers that see." Another designer adds, "Up-and-coming designers should always keep their eyes on the newest and hottest designers. As a matter of habit, they should read fashion publications and online magazines such as *Women's Wear Daily*."

Some designers also begin their careers as freelancers. However, one source warns, "Freelance jobs, especially in New York City, tend to be short-term – no more than ten months. Companies like people who are fresh and ready for training. Ironically, the more experience you have, the harder it is to find a job."

Designers stationed in large companies and design companies often have an easier time moving up the ranks. Claims a source: "Opportunities arise during expansion. Smaller companies may not take on more work. And if they are not taking on more work, people remain within their set roles. That means low growth opportunity." She continues, "The industry is getting smaller. A lot of places are closing down. Newcomers to the field need to have savvy as well as patience."

Common jobs for fresh-out-of-school fashion lovers include assistant designer and assistant technical designer. According to insiders, assistant designers are involved in sketching, flat sketches, assisting the designer and preparing the presentation material for the line. They may also assist in sourcing fabric and trim, helping the designer get the line ready and other preliminary presentations before the line is even made. In contrast, assistant technical designers assist the technical designer in grading garments, coming up with prototypes, doing spec sheets and generally taking the creative concept to the production stage. A contact classifies technical designers and their assistants as "people who are interested in design, but who are not creative designers by nature."

On the Job

An associate designer from a small company says her work varies from day to day. She may "design a new line, make presentation boards, research the market or meet with print, fabric and color studios." Sample work, or doing paperwork for the creation of sample designs, is also common. All of this hard work can be time consuming. "I may work 9 a.m. to 11 p.m. a few weeks to a few months each season," says an insider. "I'll do whatever it takes to get the job done." Besides the time commitment, other downers include dealing with bureaucracy, enduring competition and pressure, conforming to rigid company structures, keeping up with new trends and thinking about cost considerations before creativity. Fortunately, say insiders, the glories of design compensate for the difficulties. "It's so satisfying to see your work in stores," proclaims one gleeful designer.

Pay and Perks

Like many fashion professionals, designers love to see their work metamorphose from sketch to tangible creation. "It's an exhilarating feeling," declares a source. Free and heavily discounted clothes are another perk. By New York City standards, the pay scale for designers is roughly as follows: $22,000 to $30,000 for assistant and entry-level designers, $30,000 to $45,000 for associates; and $60,000 to $150,000 and up for full-fledged designers. Patternmakers' salaries begin at $25,000, but salaries for talented patternmakers may increase to $60,000 to $100,000 or more after five years. Designers that command high salaries have quite a few years of experience and talent. For real stars, the sky's the limit. Some companies tie a salary and profit/sales incentive to their designers. The incentive may be based on a small percentage of profits or sales for the company.

Vault Day in the Life: Noverto Gonzalez
Assistant Product Manager, Federated Merchandising Group

Noverto Gonzales graduated from the University of North Texas with a BA in Merchandising in 1999. His first summer internship was at J.C Penney in Texas. It was a ten-week program: five weeks as assistant department manager on the retail floor and five weeks as an assistant buyer. He knew he wanted to live in New York City, so the summer before he graduated, Noverto landed another internship in the city. He was offered an internship at Barney's and Saks Fifth Avenue but chose the one at Saks since a salary came with it. The Barney's internship paid a small stipend at the end of the summer. His New York City job search was entirely self-directed.

After graduation, he was offered a position at J.C. Penney (in Texas) and Saks Fifth Avenue. J.C. Penney was very supportive and knew he wanted to go to New York. He began his career as an assistant buyer at Saks Fifth Avenue Catalog. He moved on to Federated as an assistant product manager. Federated operates Bloomingdale's, Macy's West and East, Goldsmith's, The Bon Marche, Burdines, Lazarus and Rich's department stores. At the Federated Merchandising Group, he worked with other product managers, buyers, the design team and the technical design team. Federated Merchandising Group, a division of Federated Department Stores, is responsible for the conceptualization, design, sourcing and marketing of private brands which are exclusive to Macy's, Rich's, Lazarus, Goldsmith's, The Bon Marche, Burdines and Bloomingdale's. These private labels include: INC, Style & Co., Alfani, Tools of the Trade, Charter Club, JM Collection, Tasso Elba, Club Room and Greendog.

Noverto's Day

9:00 a.m.: Get into office and check email. Our overseas office in Turkey has left me some notes. Update production time and action plans. The approvals for fit samples, lap dips and trims are managed by product development. For example, if our designer doesn't like a button on a sample, we have to find a replacement.

10:30 a.m.: Fit model comes in. We have fittings three times a week. I keep a "Fit" book and take notes of things that were changed. The designer and assistant designer are also in the meeting.

Visit Vault at **www.vault.com** for insider company profiles, expert advice, career message boards, expert resume reviews, the Vault Job Board and more.

VAULT CAREER LIBRARY   31

11:30 a.m.: I go back to my office to update the open purchase orders. If the parameters of the order change, I have to update it and make sure the legal documents are correct as well. Some of essential information is color, style number, vendor, country of origin, first cost and landed cost. I also deal with quota issues.

12:30 p.m.: Get back to the office and work on design samples. Go over current season sales and look through styles and colors. Look at different types of bodies or fabrication. Often, I have to address costing issues. If we want our cost of production to be something specific, like $5, we might have to negotiate with our vendors. Or we would look at the price of a set and then increase the price of the pant and decrease the shirt. Every year we are pressured to reduce cost from last year.

2:00 p.m.: Grab a quick and late lunch.

2:30 p.m.: Attend line development meeting. We're always working on three seasons at once. Develop fall, go into meeting for holiday, and check spring production calendar. The seasons Federated followed were Fall, Holiday, Spring and Summer.

4:00 p.m.: Check e-mail and update my calendar. Once a week, I track all shipments. I reconcile the shipping logs, purchase orders and sales. If the shipment does not have a corresponding receipt number, I ask someone in the D.C. (distribution center) or e-mail a vendor and ask for proof of shipment.

5:30 p.m.: Track advertising samples. These samples are used for our ads. The buyers request ad samples.

6:00 p.m.: Go home!

Noverto comments: "My favorite part of the industry is working with fashion forecasting offices. You know what's going on next year. The ironic thing is that there are so many trends but most things end up looking the same! Every company does similar things. The worst part of the industry is that it is pretentious. You always have to stay on top. If something doesn't sell then you're responsible for it."

Vault Profile: Michael Hong

Director of Product Development, Kenneth Cole

Michael graduated with an Associate of Applied Science (AAS) degree in Menswear from the Fashion Institute of Technology. He continued to Cornell and left with a B.S. in Business Management. At the time, he decided that he would not be happy crunching numbers or managing people. Instead, Michael had a burning desire to create something. He began as a freelance designer at Polo Ralph Lauren and stayed for two years full-time as an assistant designer. His philosophy was that if you are going to be good, then you should focus on one area. He chose outerwear (includes jackets, hats, gloves, etc.), which is one of the most complicated.

He moved on to Andrew Marc, an outerwear company known for the quality and fashion of its leather. Michael spent five years at Andrew Marc, where he dealt with leather quality, silhouette, lining and aesthetic details. He traveled to Korea often to source new leather. "Korea used to be very well known for its leather," says Michael, "but most leather production has now shifted to China, Indonesia, and Vietnam. Samples are still made in Korea, but the product is made in China." Most companies never deal directly with the factories. Instead, they use agents who represent many different factories. Says Michael, "Until we place an order, we don't know what factory we're using."

In 2000, Michael became the Director of Product Development of Men's Outerwear at Kenneth Cole. Most mornings, he begins his day with vendor appointments to look at leather and fabric. He's in charge, so he oversees the designers and keeps them headed toward the same goals. His job is to delegate, coordinate, and keep the design team inspired. The team is designing for a full year ahead. Outerwear has a longer timeline than most clothing. In addition to his creative responsibilities, Michael oversees the technical issues as well. Before a jacket can go into production, he must approve the fit, color and fabric.

Twice a year, Michael goes to shop in Europe and look for inspiration. "Europe is about a year or two ahead of the styles in the United States," he says. "America is very mainstream, so we go to see something new. This year we hit London, Paris, Milan and Berlin."

Michael says the best part about being a designer is "when you feel in control of your creative and aesthetic talent and can see monetary gains

Visit Vault at **www.vault.com** for insider company profiles, expert advice, career message boards, expert resume reviews, the Vault Job Board and more.

VAULT CAREER LIBRARY   **33**

as a result. You know that you've made money for the company. What is perceived as good to you also makes money for the company." On the flip side, Michael says the worst part of his job is "working with untalented people who perceive themselves to be talented. And they are so insecure of their own talent that they try to undermine other people's work. It's all 'very Dynasty.'" His other dislike of the industry is "when people are nasty to other people. It's difficult to meet those people and work with them. These people are control freaks. We're not saving lives but they act like they are. Their intensity level is that of 'someone may *die* because the button is too shiny!' I can't deal with that."

He agrees that designing is extremely subjective. There is never one ultimate right answer. Michael continues, "We're working with a target market that's moving. It becomes guesswork. To stay current, I listen to a lot of music. What's current is what the music industry is doing. It's always been and it always will be."

Manufacturing

Manufacturing refers to the process of converting fabric, trims, and designs into a finished product, especially by means of a large-scale industrial operation. Not all clothing manufacturers create every piece of the garment. Many manufacturers are design houses that contract out the actual sewing of the garment. By 2005, when the U.S. relaxes its import quotas, many manufacturers will contract actual production of the garments overseas. However, manufacturers will still face tariff charges on imported garments.

Jobs

Fabric buyer: Purchases the appropriate fabrics for production. Manages delivery, negotiates costs, and oversees fabric issues.

Import/Export specialist: Keeps up with trade laws in order to ensure that supplies are from the most cost-efficient sources.

Operator: Performs one or more sewing steps in the general creation of the garment.

Production manager: Oversees the operations involved in garment manufacturing and ensures that all workers are on schedule.

Production pattern maker: Revamps the sample patterns so that they are easier to produce.

Quality control person: Ensures that the produced garments are of the appropriate size, quality and composition.

Trim buyer: Scouts out the top suppliers of buttons, zippers and miscellaneous pieces that hold a garment together.

The Scoop

Production processes vary, but the majority of production work is technical in nature. The key to production is synchronicity, insiders say. Employees must be more than efficient; they must also stay on schedule with the rest of the production crew. Production managers monitor the training, machinery and efficiency of each employee. Essentially, they make sure that employees are on track with their individual job responsibilities. These responsibilities might include coordinating fabric deliveries to and from factories, scheduling

Visit Vault at **www.vault.com** for insider company profiles, expert advice, career message boards, expert resume reviews, the Vault Job Board and more.

VAULT CAREER LIBRARY   35

shipments, arranging raw materials for construction, creating work schedules and tracking services, deliveries and orders. Because of the amount of scheduling and coordination, employees in supervisory roles tend to be well organized and detail-oriented. Strong customer service abilities are also essential. If the company buys or sells internationally, coordinators must understand the legal issues surrounding importing, exporting and the U.S. Customs Department.

Production workers typically specialize in one or more aspects of the industry: sewing, cutting, bundling, fabric spreading, packing, finishing or pattern making. While production is not a high-profile area of fashion, it is nevertheless essential. Without a production plan, patterns are simply paper and designers merely dreamers. For production to succeed, each employee must complete his or her job in a timely manner. One inefficient worker can throw the entire team off schedule. Late or failed deliveries of items can also lead to scheduling problems and cancelled retailers' orders. In short, a well-oiled, efficient and team-oriented production staff is the backbone of any successful fashion company.

Getting Hired

Production is one area of fashion that is always in need of fresh talent. In fact, insiders report that the most difficult positions for them to fill are production-related; these include sewing machine operators, production managers, spreaders and cutters. Employees in production have a distinct career path. For example, cutters become pattern cutters and eventually cutting room managers. Sewing machine operators can work their way up to sample sewing, where they work closely with the design team. Many fashion industry insiders also say that production serves as a great background for design work. At a few high-end design companies, such as Vera Wang, production may actually help with design.

Pay and Perks

One source says that the apparel industry in New York generates more than $20 billion a year in revenue, making it the city's largest manufacturing sector. Nevertheless, wages can be meager – and even close to the poverty level at some manufacturing companies. According to one survey, the average annual wage for an apparel-manufacturing employee (such as sewing or cutting) was a low $17,600. Entry-level production employees (such as assistant trim buyers or import assistants) earn $25,000 to 30,000. Production managers may earn $60,000 to $150,000 after many years of experience. Employees at manufacturers can typically buy overstock, samples, and returned or damaged clothing for less than wholesale price. Some companies have warehouse sales that only employees and family are allowed to attend.

Vault Day in the Life: Karen Lott

Fabric Buyer, BCBG

Karen Lott has over 25 years of experience in the industry. She attended Pasadena City College and graduated with an associate degree in Merchandise Management. She began her career at the May Company as a salesperson and worked her way to Assistant Manager and then Department Manager. At that point, Karen moved from retail to corporate and became an assistant buyer. She moved to a missy company (the missy category usually includes a more womanly, more shapely fit, as opposed to a juniors fit) and started as assistant to the Sales Manager and was eventually promoted to Executive Vice President. After a few years, she decided to take a new job with less responsibility. Since then, she has held several positions as a piece goods buyer.

She has worked at BCBG for several years as the piece goods buyer. The biggest challenge at BCBG was adapting to constant change. "Since the company defines contemporary hip, we have to have the coolest product," Karen says. "For production, you need level-headed people to handle the stress of the job. However, people who are ingrained in their jobs have a tough time with change. What happens in a company like BCBG is that there is huge turnover in personnel in certain areas like design. Kids coming out of F.I.T. think BCBG is the hip, cool place to work and want it on their resume. So they get it on their resume and leave. Turnover is high for pattern makers and design assistants, and you see want ads for those positions all the time. On the other hand, you rarely see ads for production people – they have been there for a long time."

Over the past 25 years, according to Karen, the most significant change in the fashion industry has been the "dramatic increase in import production." "Years ago, there was more loyalty in the business but fewer options. Now, if you are looking for a particular fabric or trim, the options are endless," she says. "Buying fabric is a truly international

Visit Vault at **www.vault.com** for insider company profiles, expert advice, career message boards, expert resume reviews, the Vault Job Board and more.

VAULT CAREER LIBRARY

37

and collaborative experience. My job requires me to work with planning (which tells me what yardage to buy of every individual fabric), fabric sourcing (which tells me what vendor to purchase the fabric from), production managers (who advise on delivery status of fabric), L.C. and trafficking (where I submit shipping documents and track fabric through freight forwarder) and accounts payable (so I can check requests and wire transfers).

Karen's Day

9:00 a.m.: Turn computer on and check e-mails. Typically, I have 60 e-mails from vendors in Turkey, Italy, Hong Kong, Hungary or even nearby in New York City. The e-mails usually contain information about fabric delivery and financing. I respond to the e-mails that I have answers to immediately and then move onto to my voice mails. Once the fabrics arrive in Los Angeles, my responsibilities do not end. I have to monitor quality control issues and work with the warehouse manager to manage the inventory.

10:00 a.m.: Meet up with the planners. Part of my job is to work with the planning department. At BCBG, I work with three different planners that buy for the Knit, Woven and Dress departments. At one point, I also bought fabric for swimwear, Nordstrom's and Men's departments. Eventually, those departments closed down.

11:00 a.m.: Run to production meetings. The Knit, Woven and Dress departments each have their own production manager – which means I often have to go to three different production meetings. Each meeting is one to three hours so some days I am stuck in meetings all day. I ask, "When is fabric shipping? When do you expect it to be in factory? How is it being financed?" I am prepared to answer pattern and trim status on every individual style in production. We must address design challenges and delivery dates of finished garments already in production. We run through the meeting by delivery dates. For example, we cover April deliveries first, May deliveries next, and anything beyond that last. Sometimes we are quite a few months ahead.

2:00 p.m.: Submit documents for opening of Letters of Credit (L.C.). L.C.s are used for international sales. They are drawn up by a bank and are a recognized financial instrument designed to protect the buyer and seller in international dealings. The L.C. describes in detail the items to be purchased (condition and number of items, insurance, inspection etc.) and states the conditions of payment to the seller (when and how the amounts are payable). The L.C. is only honored when all conditions have been met, as checked by both my and the seller's banks. It is my responsibility to ensure the L.C. is open and in place.

3:00 p.m.: Follow through with open L.C.s and payment.

4:00 p.m.: I usually skip lunch to get work done. For our Korean suppliers, we have to show proof of payment before they export. All Korean orders have to have a Korean insurance agency (KEIC – Korean insurance export company) as well. Our Korean vendors require post-dated checks before the fabric is released from the dock.

4:30 p.m.: Track L.C. requests. For any purchase order, I request a check. Each check requires two signatures (Pre-Production VP and Executive VP) before Accounts Payable would issue the check. Checks could be small or as much as $50,000.

5:00 p.m.: Check with our warehouse to coordinate fabric delivery. Some fabric arrives from Italy for local production. I go over the inspection reports and approve it for production since it looks normal. When there are problems, I go over to the warehouse to inspect the fabric myself. If there is a problem with the fabric, I have to decide how much of it is salvageable. Then I have to deal with the vendor for charge backs and returns. I work with the warehouse manager and quality control on a daily basis.

7:30 p.m.: Go home! Save my new voice mails for tomorrow.

Visit Vault at **www.vault.com** for insider company profiles, expert advice, career message boards, expert resume reviews, the Vault Job Board and more.

VAULT CAREER LIBRARY

39

How is a Garment Created?

Stage 1: Fiber & Yarn

All garments begin as fiber. Fibers are fine, flexible and threadlike filaments. The two basic types of fibers are natural fibers (such as cotton, wool, linen and silk) and man-made fibers (such as nylon, polyester, rayon, acetate, spandex and acrylic). Yarns can be single fibers or many varieties of fibers twisted together. If you read a content label on a garment, you will see that these yarns do not necessarily make up a single garment. Within one garment, it is possible to have cashmere, silk and nylon yarns, for example. Textile designers choose specific yarns to give a garment specific characteristics. For example, a garment made with cashmere is extremely soft, while a garment that contains spandex has stretch. These yarns are then combined together to make a fabric.

Stage 2: Fabric

Garments are made from yarns that are knit or woven together. Knit fabrics are produced on knitting machines, whereas woven fabrics are made on a loom. In general, knit fabrics are used most often in sportswear because knits tend to be more comfortable with natural stretch. Wovens are more commonly used in dress shirts, coats or trousers since the fabric has a little more structure. After the yarns are knit or woven, the fabric must still be subjected to dyeing and chemical treatments to give it the proper feel and texture. When the fabric is finished, it is inspected for shrinkage, color, smoothness and various industry standards. For example, in infant wear, fabrics are required to meet stringent flammability requirements for the infant's safety.

Stage 3: Manufacturing

The fabric is received at the manufacturers' warehouse, and it is usually sent out for cutting. Cutting involves layers upon layers of fabric stacked on each other with pattern pieces laid out on top like a jigsaw puzzle. These pattern pieces include the entire range of the size scale and are arranged using computer systems so that every square inch of the fabric is used – leaving less than 5 percent of the fabric wasted. The fabric is cut and "bundled" together with similar pieces. The bundled pieces are then sent to the sewing plant along with other parts of the garment, such as zippers and buttons, also known as trim. Trim usually reaches the sewing plant separately. In the sewing plant, the cut panels are stitched into a garment and the trim is added. A garment may then undergo dyeing, washing or some other specialized process. For example, jeans may be enzymed (in which chemicals are applied to make the garment feel softer), bleached, sandblasted and stonewashed. After this process, the garment may have embroidery, screenprint or some other embellishment added as a last step. Typical embellishments may include logos, artwork or even beading.

The garment is now finished. However, it is not ready to sell. The sewn garment goes through a final step that includes quality control and packaging. The garment is inspected and, if it passes, it is folded, ticketed and pressed. The ticket usually contains the Universal Product Code (UPC) in the form of a barcode, price and vendor.

Stage 4: Retailer

The manufacturer can ship the garments to a distribution center or directly to a store. At the distribution center, the clothes may be unpacked and inspected. Nationwide retailers may have a few distribution hubs scattered around the country, whereas other retailers may not have one at all. A catalog usually has only one distribution center, since all the garments are shipped directly to the consumer after purchase. At this point, the garment is considered "floor-ready." After the retail store receives shipments, the store might not unpack the cartons for a few days to sort and prepare the garments for display. Once the items are on the retail floor, the garments may be on the floor for 30 to 90 days before a consumer purchases them.

Visit Vault at www.vault.com for insider company profiles, expert advice, career message boards, expert resume reviews, the Vault Job Board and more.

VAULT CAREER LIBRARY   41

Use the Internet's
MOST TARGETED
job search tools.

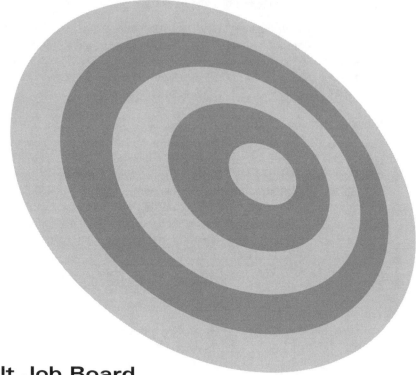

Vault Job Board

Target your search by industry, function, and experience level, and find the job openings that you want.

VaultMatch Resume Database

Vault takes match-making to the next level: post your resume and customize your search by industry, function, experience and more. We'll match job listings with your interests and criteria and e-mail them directly to your inbox.

Buying and Merchandising

CHAPTER 7

Buying and merchandising refers to the process by which stores purchase merchandise from wholesalers and, in turn, sell it to customers. Buyers select products that reflect hot trends for their markets. A buyer for a boutique is very different than a buyer for a department store. A buyer for a boutique may rely more on fashion trends and vendor suggestions. A buyer for a department store may analyze past sales for the store, profit margins and cost of goods sold information before they place an order. Merchandisers promote the sale of garments. They may work with designers, salespeople, or retailers. A merchandiser may advise salespeople how to sell or display the product. Like designers, all buyers and merchandisers begin as assistants.

Jobs

Assistant buyer: Assists the buyer in the purchase and tracking of merchandise.

Buyer: Purchases the appropriate merchandise for the store's customers.

Assistant merchandiser: Helps merchandiser successfully promote product.

Merchandiser: Develops and implements the product line. Must be able to communicate with customers as well as coordinate with sales team.

Stylist: A designer of, or consultant on, styles in decorating, dress or beauty. A stylist is most often employed for advertisements.

The Scoop

Among fashion jobs, buying is arguably the most intense, tiring and rewarding. Many buyers claim that "previous store experience is an asset," since it helps them understand the consumer. Other buyers, however, believe that retail experience is not paramount. "If you're going to be a buyer at Macy's or Lord & Taylor," suggests an insider, "it's not necessary to have store experience because they will train you anyway." One contact states that an inexperienced Macy's trainee can become a buyer in only three to five years.

While department stores offer the benefit of systematic training, specialty stores often operate on a different track. At Polo, relates another insider, "you may have ten people running the whole show," suggests a source. "That

Visit Vault at **www.vault.com** for insider company profiles, expert advice, career message boards, expert resume reviews, the Vault Job Board and more.

VAULT CAREER LIBRARY 43

means one buyer and one assistant buyer making all the decisions. At a private designer you do a lot more right from the beginning – but just how much is dependent upon your boss." In general, smaller companies assign buyers a wider ranger of responsibilities. On the other hand, buying jobs at department stores "are known to be less creative and more analytical."

In buying, the job progression goes from assistant buyer to associate buyer and, finally, to buyer. Buyers often come from computer, math, economics or business backgrounds. They differ from traditional fashion professionals in that they often prefer analytical skills over creativity. Perhaps a buyer's most vital assets are math skills, negotiation abilities, a forthright personality and management and organizational skills. Buyers tend to have a working knowledge of mark-ups and markdowns, gross margins, inventory control and turnover relationships, merchandise plans and vendor relations, along with other general accounting. Explains one buyer: "The buyer is, in many senses, an entrepreneur. Both my assistant and I must be able to communicate effectively. We must be able to speak up and to think on our feet."

On the road

Marketing is one function of a buyer's job; analysis and store visitations are others. A background in retail comes in handy with store visits. Buyers must pay attention to how their company's merchandise is being displayed, what colors and sizes are available and where and how other competitors' merchandise is displayed.

Since most major brands offer locations throughout the U.S., it is not unusual for a buyer to spend substantial time on the road. Frequent travel, combined with rigorous hours, makes buying an exhausting profession. "Buyers have to go to stores on the weekends. They need a pulse about what's going on in the 'real world.' Buyers also visit stores on holidays, especially around Christmas." All that traveling inspires not only fatigue, but also high turnover. After several years, many a burnt-out buyer will move to another, less time-intensive job within the fashion industry.

Collaboration

Buyers frequently collaborate with other groups within merchandising. As such, weekly meetings with the whole merchandising department are the norm. The department may discuss upcoming sales, new strategies or targeted goals. Explains one buyer, "For Memorial Day weekend, we might discuss which merchandise will go on sale. We'll talk about the possibilities of a combined sale and how best to promote our goods in order to achieve our overall sales target." Buyers are trying to make not only their individual sales targets, but also the sales targets of the entire company. This dual aim leads to intense pressure that motivates some buyers and drains others. "My company holds its buyers accountable for its plans and sales targets. I'm always aware that my actions can make or break the company as a whole," confesses one buyer. "The pressure doesn't abate month to month because if I don't make my sales target, then the CEO has to go back to the shareholders and explain why." He concludes, "You don't get to a buyer position unless you understand the rules and play the game well."

Many buyers also experience what are known as Open Buy Weekends; these generally take place once a month. Open Buy Weekends offer a forum for all major company representatives. Buyers approach Open Buy Weekends by preparing reports on sales and revenue. Shares a buyer: "I'll go to the meeting and say that I'm either on target, overbought or underbought. If I'm over- or underbought, I'll need to explain why. Often, the managers are already aware of the possibility of underperforming sales. However, if the problem comes as a surprise, that's very bad. I may have to cancel an order from a vendor. I may even lose my job because, in essence, I'm playing with the company's money."

Getting Hired

Some fashion buying programs recruit at undergraduate institutions. Our contacts say that the interview makes or breaks prospective buyers. Because most employees will begin as associate or assistant buyers, a good rapport with the senior buyer is crucial. One contact in the field says he looks for the following when hiring an assistant: "I want someone who is smart. This person doesn't need to know everything, but they must be able to learn and to learn quickly. I want someone who takes notes. It's no good telling someone a piece of information only to have him come back a few hours later unable to remember it. Write it down!"

The number of interviews for any buying position will depend on several factors: experience level, job title and the interviewer's impression of the candidate, among others. Because buying is often quantitative in nature, interviewees should expect to receive questions during the interview that test math ability. At Neiman Marcus, prospective buyers must take a retail math test as part of the interview. "Don't be afraid if you can't do the problem in your head," reveals a source. "My company hired one woman after she

Visit Vault at **www.vault.com** for insider company profiles, expert advice, career message boards, expert resume reviews, the Vault Job Board and more.

VAULT CAREER LIBRARY   **45**

explained she wasn't very good at math and pulled out a calculator. As you can see, the ability to think on one's feet is essential." Of course, traditional analytical and "fit" questions also apply. Another insider explains, "I always ask my applicants, 'What is the toughest decision you have ever had to make?' I don't care very much about the answer, but I do watch to see how they react, how they think things through."

Pay and Perks

A buyer's salary will range depending upon experience level, company, product category, and location. In New York, a seasoned worker may make between $60,000 and $80,000, while a first-time buyer may only earn around $35,000. Outside of "the fashion capital of the world," however, buyer salaries may be substantially lower. On the other hand, perks in buying are often generous. One insider claims he receives "company discounts of 50 percent (and even more at warehouse sales), as well as free watches, umbrellas and other accessories." A successful merchandiser will bring home $60,000 to $150,000 a year.

Vault Day in the Life: Buyer at DKNY

8:00 a.m.: Arrive at work. Take a look at the sales. "You're concerned with the breakdown of items sold at each store: how many dress shirts, ties, trousers and so on. Buyers are constantly asking themselves 'Why did one store sell many more than the other?' Maybe the display might be different. Maybe one store did a sale. It depends. You need to find out."

10:00 a.m.: Consult with the assistant buyer. Make sure he or she is on track with various deals and operations.

11:00 a.m.: Spend time on sales analysis – "You do some yourself, delegate some to the assistant buyer."

("Certain days are spent entirely on analysis. It's very important to know retail math and to understand concepts like the 'gross product margin.' It's okay for an assistant buyer to not know retail math at first, but he must learn quickly!")

1:30 p.m.: Go out to lunch with a friend. Relax for half an hour.

2:00 p.m.: Attend a buyers' meeting. ("During a major buyers' meeting, all buyers will come in – from Bloomingdale's, Polo, you name it. They'll discuss what's coming up for the next fashion season – styles, colors and sizes. They'll also discuss who will be doing production and how the garments will be delivered.")

4:30 p.m.: Review the notes I typed on my laptop during the meeting.

5:00 p.m.: Meet with my assistant for a review of the meeting.

6:00 p.m.: Plan a store visit for tomorrow ("Marketing is one aspect of buyer life, analysis is another, and visiting stores is still another. It's important to see how things are being merchandised and displayed.")

7:00 p.m.: Grab a snack – maybe some fruit and a bagel. Do more sales analysis.

8:00 p.m.: Leave work to enjoy dinner and a quiet, low-key night.

Vault Day in the Life: Sylvia Dundon

Dress Buyer, Victoria's Secret Catalog

Sylvia Dundon graduated from the Fashion Institute of Technology with a BA in Marketing (concentration Merchandising Management) and an AAS. Buying and Merchandising in December 1998. It took two years to obtain her AAS and another three years for her BA since she was working at the Gap and Victoria's Secret while she was attending school. She began her career as an Assistant Buyer at Victoria's Secret Catalog and later was promoted to Associate Buyer.

Sylvia's Day

9:00 a.m.: Check e-mail and voice mail. Prioritize who gets called back first based on what time zone they're in.

9:30 a.m.: Check sales on computer – especially dress sales for the items I bought most recently. If the catalog just dropped (that is, was sent out), wait a few days for the sales to hit. Work with the planner. ("At Victoria's Secret, the planner is the buyer's partner. The planner executes the actual purchase order, financial planning, stock models, and markdowns.")

10:30 a.m.: Decide how to allocate five pages of the catalog. For example, how many dresses should I feature per page? Do I think I'll

Visit Vault at **www.vault.com** for insider company profiles, expert advice, career message boards, expert resume reviews, the Vault Job Board and more.

VAULT CAREER LIBRARY   47

sell more dresses with three per page or should I focus on one large picture of a single dress? I have to justify my decisions to management and work with merchandise manager. Some of my decisions are based on what sold in the catalog last year.

11:30 a.m.: Sample fitting. Go to the fit room and work with your technical specialist and fit model. The fit model tries on samples and we make sure the garment is the right specifications and fit. If the garment is not correct, we send our corrections to the vendor. A sample garment usually goes through one to three rounds of corrections.

12:00 p.m.: Layout and film review. I go visit the Creative Department and look at a layout of our catalog. The point is to review the actual photography and layout (for colors). If the color of the garment is wrong, I cut a swatch from the garment as a sample so the Creative Dept. can fix the photo to match. If the skirt in the photo is too long, they can fix the length, too. If everything looks great, I just approve the layout.

12:45 p.m.: Run out to buy a sandwich so I can eat at my desk and check voice mail.

2:00 p.m.: Roll out my sample rack. Send out samples for a photo shoot. Work with in-house model for shoot samples to make sure they fit and look right according to Victoria's Secret standards.

3:00 p.m.: Meet a few vendors. I cut a few fabric swatches for product development. Sometimes I go out into the market or vendor showrooms to look at their lines. If I really like something, I will ask them to send samples for me the next day.

4:00 p.m.: Go to a fashion forecast meeting. This meeting includes both the fashion and design departments and is intended to make sure that we're all aware of the trends and direction that Victoria's Secret wants to take that season. Even though we're buying different categories (dresses, shirts, etc.), we all want to have the same mindset. I also see slide shows of samples bought in Europe. All the buyers get to see the main themes for the season – which include a color palette and the general trends.

6:00 p.m.: Address production issues. Approve a button or lab dip. The lap dip is the color intended for production. Quite often, the manufacturer hasn't produced the correct color, so I have to ask them to do another lab dip.

7:00 p.m.: Address the e-mails I didn't get to during the day. Go home!

Retail

Retail covers the sale of apparel and related goods and services in small quantities directly to consumers. In the rush for fashion jobs, the retail sector has emerged as a promising contender. Sears, Roebuck and Co., for example, has created the "Retail Executive Development Training Program" to recruit promising new professionals. Considered a retail milestone by many, the program targets 60 undergraduate campuses. After an eight- to 10-month training program, "executive trainees" handle up to $3 million in profit/loss responsibility. Some trainees have as many as 30 people reporting to them. Retailers such as Sears, Neiman Marcus, Federated and Meryvn's offer candidates a nice deal – signficant management responsibility in a relatively short amount of time.

Some larger retail programs have established training programs. The Gap hires recent college graduates for its Retail Management Program. The program is based in San Francisco over a seven-month period. New hires gain experience in merchandising, planning and production. After successfully completing the program, the graduates have an opportunity to work full-time in the brand (i.e. Old Navy, Banana Republic, Gap Baby, etc.) in which they trained – and are placed based on Gap's needs, as well as each graduate's skills and interests. The Gap offers other programs to recent college graduates such as the College Manager in Training. The College Manager in Training (CMIT) program is a formal six-month process that takes new managers through all facets of running a Gap, Banana Republic or Old Navy store. Check the Gap corporate website for more information. Their contact information is:

Gap Inc. Campus Relations
2 Folsom Street
San Francisco, CA 94105
Fax: (415) 427-6804
Email: college_recruiting@gap.com

Jobs

Retail clerk: Assists the consumer in the purchase of products and services.

Store manager: Manages the store operations and supervises the clerks.

Marketing: Works on store advertisements and catalogs.

Inventory planner: Sets monetary limits on the retail buyers' purchasing power based on historical and market analysis.

Asset protection: Minimizes store losses and track fraud and theft.

Logistics: Works with stores and buyers to optimize supply-chain.

Real estate: Manages stores that vary in size, location, and layout to keep stores new. Responsibilities may include construction and building services management.

The Scoop

Many people have a less-than-positive view of retailing. "I didn't spend four years in college to work in a store!" is a frequent gripe. This negative reaction belies the fact that retail is a good place to start or build a fashion career. Because jobs selling fine design can be extremely lucrative, retail is becoming more attractive to college graduates. Larger stores are often the best places to start since some offer standardized training programs. Comments an insider: "One of retail's biggest problems is that there is no standard training pattern. Many retailers wait for people to get on the-job-training elsewhere and then cannibalize their competitors." Despite the problem of unstructured training, retail has one indisputably stellar element: almost anyone is eligible. "We look for employees with bachelor's degrees," says an industry source. "School isn't very important. Major isn't very important. Many people who specialized in business, finance or liberal arts will do just fine."

On the corporate side of fashion, opportunities exist in retail buying, planning, merchandising and product development. College grads typically start out as trainees and work their way up, following established or somewhat meandering career paths. Talented and dedicated new hires, especially in large companies or department stores, can expect regular promotions – up to divisional management roles. There are also opportunities in store management, finance and human resources. More creative jobs in retail include catalog production (graphics and copywriting) and window and display design.

Image

While some insiders laud department stores, others attest to the value of small designer companies. "Department stores are out," declares one adamant source. "Smaller, more prestigious retailers – CK, Armani, Tommy Hilfiger – are the way to go. Department stores are stuffy and they convey a feeling of being 'average.' The people I know working on the selling floor of department stores want to get out." Underlying this comment are issues of prestige and class, two prominent – although seldom discussed – aspects of retail. Fashion, and retail in particular, is an image-conscious sector in which an attractive appearance, up-to-date style, impeccable grooming and an air of affluence are important. "High-end retail is a glamour job," says an insider. "The positions are high-profile and low-paying. The people who work in retail are often highly educated and parentally subsidized. The job becomes a lifestyle of fashionable wardrobes, cocktail parties, elite crowds and making the right friends." If you detect an edge of superficiality, insiders confirm it. "High-end retail jobs are often aimed at high-class young women," says a source. "They deal with a wealthy and prominent clientele. Some of the girls are old school – out to find a rich husband."

Employees may have to invest thousands of dollars on a wardrobe to wear to work. In fact, most high-end retailers require their employees to wear only their label. One contact at Ralph Lauren says she must have her work apparel approved by the company, a cumbersome and expensive process. "For a job that pays by the hour," explains a contact, "you may have to invest quite a bit of money." This dress can be very expensive, even though employees receive discounts and supplementary commissions.

Fortunately, selling takes on new meaning when employees are dealing with celebrities and high-powered execs with money to burn. Those who excel in retail know how to build relationships with their customers – "setting aside" new arrivals or sending cards and little gifts (paid for by the company, of course). Wealthy clients may need pampering, but the insiders say the money compensates for the labor. "We're talking about people who walk into a store and buy the same outfit in five different colors," says an insider.

Getting Hired

Retail hiring managers say they look for applicants with the following traits: integrity, the ability to develop and grow within the business, the desire to relate with and accommodate the customer, business knowledge, good reading and writing skills, company loyalty, extraordinary interpersonal skills and a cheerful attitude and disposition. These traits, sources say, are often much more important than schooling or even previous retail training. As with any fashion job – or job in general – good interviewing skills, knowledge of

Visit Vault at **www.vault.com** for insider company profiles, expert advice, career message boards, expert resume reviews, the Vault Job Board and more.

VAULT CAREER LIBRARY **51**

the industry and an understanding of the hiring company are the magical ingredients to landing a position.

Pay and Perks

While entry-level salaries vary quite drastically within retail, trainees at large companies and department stores report annual earnings of approximately $30,000. Once they move up the corporate chain, many of these trainees can look forward to twice that much money in three to five years. Commissions add up – and retail salespeople with exceptional fashion sense and people skills can rake in juicy salaries. Some insiders in retail report earnings as high as $100,000 a year. Other perks? Insiders from more flashy and prestigious companies report invitations to parties, resorts, shows and posh summer homes.

Vault Day in the Life: Inventory Planner at an International Retail Label

9:00 a.m.: Arrive to work and look over notes from a meeting on the previous day. ("It isn't surprising that planners sit in on a lot of meetings.")

9:30 a.m.: Work with buyers on fashion forecasts and changes to the company's budget. ("You will work very closely with buyers. For example, if they need more money for a project, you will rearrange the budget.")

12:30 p.m.: Break for lunch. Take a short walk.

1:15 p.m.: Meet with the VP of Merchandising to do analysis on a recent line.

3:00 p.m.: Attend a company-wide meeting on the company's status and direction. ("There can be a meeting every hour at this company. That's not unusual. Fortunately, with so many projects in the works, your days are always different.")

4:00 p.m.: Speak with a designer about color preferences. ("The more experience you have, the more diversity you have in your tasks.

Diversity in experience adds to your potential – changes the interview questions from that of 'what can you do' to 'what do you want to do.'")

5:00 p.m.: Make changes to a budget plan – this involves some number grinding. Check the number with the buyers again.

6:00 p.m.: Run out to grab a sandwich and some caffeine. Notice what people are wearing on the street. ("You can learn about new and upcoming trends by observing fashionable people.")

6:30 p.m.: Show budget to the marketing department. ("Marketing is an up-and-coming field. Whereas it used to be done by agencies, there's a general move toward in-house marketing now. Everyone wants their name to be seen.")

7:00: Leave for the day.

Vault Day in the Life: Marketer at Federated Department Stores

7:00 a.m.: Roll out of bed, take a shower, get dressed and go to work.

8:00 a.m.: Check the sales numbers from the day before. Get nervous if there is a problem. ("After the launch of a new product, you'll know within three to four weeks whether it's going to be good or a bomb. The sales numbers let you know.")

9:30 a.m.: Make decisions about marking up and marking down various products. ("If a new product is a bomb, you mark it down – assuming that low sales aren't the result of the product being in the backroom, improperly displayed, or something like that. In this field, nobody takes responsibility for an 'ugly' product because no one is totally responsible for it – someone designed it, someone else bought that design and another person actually produced it.")

11:00 a.m.: Talk on the phone with vendors who are selling things. Lots of phoning, lots of follow-up. Also check to see how products are doing – the reception of those products. The rest of that time is spent reviewing marketing trends, including yearly financial trends.

1:30 p.m.: Eat lunch. ("Sometimes I'll go out for half an hour. A lot of the time I'm too busy, so I eat at my desk or on the run.")

Visit Vault at **www.vault.com** for insider company profiles, expert advice, career message boards, expert resume reviews, the Vault Job Board and more.

V/\ULT CAREER LIBRARY   53

2:00 p.m.: Work on random projects. Review new business opportunities, survey sales trends, perform sales and style analysis. ("Afternoons are always filled with random projects. There's no telling what – and how much – you'll have.")

4:00 p.m.: Take a call from the vice president of a major clothing manufacturer. ("A lot of my job is dealing with important people such as presidents, VPs and managers of companies.")

7:00 p.m.: Eat dinner. Grumble about the long hours. ("This job is a huge time commitment. You lose perspective after long, long days. It's also very competitive, so you're expected to stay late.")

9:00 p.m.: Leave work, exhausted but satisfied.

Cosmetics

CHAPTER 9

Cosmetics include makeup, products for the body and related goods and services. Cosmetics are meant to be rubbed, poured, sprinkled or sprayed on, or otherwise applied for cleansing, beautifying, promoting attractiveness or altering appearance. The industry is very competitive and fickle. It is also an industry with very high margins on the designer side. A successful designer perfume or cologne costs very little to produce but sells at a premium price.

Jobs

Account executive: Responsible for visiting all counter sales and doors. They explain new products and "gifts with purchase" (free items given out upon purchase of a certain cosmetics item that costs more than a set amount).

Cosmetician: Provides facial and body treatments for clients.

Counter sales: Sells cosmetics to the general public.

Freelance makeup artist: Provides clients with beauty advice and cosmetics assistance – usually paid by the cosmetic company by the hour.

Marketing: Manages research focus groups, and provides other marketing services (sales forecasting, allocation to different retailers, etc.).

Product development: Creates and refines cosmetics. Some positions that fall under this category include chemists, quality assurance and packaging people.

The Scoop

Jobs in the cosmetics industry include cosmetics counter help in department stores, direct sales (i.e., Mary Kay or Avon), makeup artists and executive positions at large companies like Estée Lauder, to name a few. There are more to managerial jobs in cosmetics than powder puffs and lip gloss. In fact, top salespeople can make six figures at a multi-level marketing company like Avon. While most jobs in the cosmetics industry are on the retail end – either selling makeup, applying makeup or managing makeup counters – there are also ample jobs in corporations for marketers, cosmetics manufacturers and others.

Visit Vault at **www.vault.com** for insider company profiles, expert advice, career message boards, expert resume reviews, the Vault Job Board and more.

VAULT CAREER LIBRARY 55

In the cosmetics industry, most new companies have entrepreneurial roots. First there was Hard Candy, the nail polish company Dineh Mohajer started in her bathroom, mixing odd-colored nail polishes in 1995. Mohajer started out with pastel and flashy colors and names like Sky, Sunshine, Gold Digger, Porno and Trailer Trash. Los Angeles starlets flocked to the unusual shades. Within a year, Hard Candy was on the shelves of high-end department stores and elite boutiques everywhere. In 1999, the luxury brand LVMH (Moët Hennessy – Louis Vuitton) purchased Hard Candy and expanded the brand's focus.

Motorola and LVMH's Hard Candy have collaborated on a co-branded cell phone. The wireless phone will be sold in Hard Candy's nail polish colors with the Hard Candy Logo, to appeal to Hard Candy's generation Y customers. The phones will come in color sets including Chump, Galaxy, Pussy Cat, Static and Space Boy. Buyers can coordinate the color of their cell phones with their nail polish.

Australia-born Poppy King caused quite a stir with her production of 1940s-inspired matte cosmetics. She continues to do business in her native country, as well as in London and Singapore. In the U.S., working mom Bobbi Brown made herself rich on a line of makeup designed for women who don't like to wear makeup – the foundations are yellow-based, for easier blending, and all her lipsticks, even her reds, are heavily muted with natural brown tones. These relative youngsters don't stay independent for long. Estee Lauder acquired Bobbi Brown Professional Cosmetics; it also acquired equity interest in trendy upstart M.A.C. (Make-up Art Cosmetics).

Getting Hired

The normal hiring rules of retail apply to cosmetics positions. However, cosmetics – perhaps more than any other retail sector – is dominated by women. Young and attractive women are often favored, since salespeople are expected to lure customers as well as to reflect the "quality" of the products. Typically, salespeople and cosmetologists use the product line so that customers can witness firsthand the products' results.

Pay and Perks

As with apparel, retail salaries in cosmetics vary dramatically. Under a multi-level marketing structure such as Revlon's, salespeople get a cut of the profits from their own sales, from the sales of the people they have recruited, and often, from the sales of recruits' recruits. However, a cosmetic sales rep in a department store may earn a set salary that is not particularly generous. Insiders remark that retail work in the cosmetics sector involves "setting and making individual target goals. Motivation and personal drive are very important."

Vault Profile: Debra Baker

Executive Director of Finance, Stila

Debra Baker joined Stila as the executive director of finance in June 2001. She graduated from the University of Michigan and also worked at Disney and estyle.com. She "sort of fell into the cosmetics industry." "One of the best parts of the cosmetics industry is that the product is easy to understand," she says. However, the most difficult aspect is that "it's hard to keep up. Everything changes so quickly. As soon as you develop a good product, everyone copies you so you have to start over." Debra adds, "You crave those times when you can have a productive day. Yet everyday, something crazy or sporadic occurs."

According to Debra, Stila is still very entrepreneurial since it's a young company. In 1994, Jeanine Lobell created the first Stila product. (In cosmetics, the companies all create their own product. Most products can be divided into treatment lines or color [a.k.a. makeup]. Treatment lines can include lotions with alpha hydroxy or retinal eye cream. Once a company develops a new treatment product, other companies follow suit. As a result, product development plays a big role. Because resources are always limited, a cosmetic company can only launch a few new products per year. Color [a.k.a. makeup] is tied in with fashion.) Stila does cutting edge color – but sometimes "it is too strong for consumers." Other times, Stila "hits it on the mark and we can't make it fast enough."

Estée Lauder bought Stila in 1999. Estée Lauder's other brands include Lauder, Aramis, Clinique, Prescriptives, Origins, MAC, La Mer, Bobbi Brown, Tommy Hilfiger, Donna Karan, Aveda, Jo Malone, Bumble and Bumble and Kate Spade Beauty. As a result, the different brands share

Visit Vault at **www.vault.com** for insider company profiles, expert advice, career message boards, expert resume reviews, the Vault Job Board and more.

VAULT CAREER LIBRARY   57

many resources and information to help one another. One of the resources that we share is the research group. The corporation has a difficult time balancing the needs of all the brands. Stila shares information with Bobbi Brown and MAC – but also competes with them. Estée Lauder isn't the only conglomerate with this problem. LVMH owns Bliss, Urban Decay, Hard Candy, BeneFit and Guerlian. "The marketplace is very cluttered with brands. It's becoming extremely difficult to distinguish the brand," laments Debra.

"Stila has very focused people," Debra says. "We create the formulas in Los Angeles and use Lauder labs for research. We have an office in every major country to work on distribution and sales. The product is basically the same in every country since it easier to manufacture a product with the same specs everywhere. Cosmetics are very universal, but countries will have different feedback on the same product." In addition, Stila will take an existing product but personalize it for that region, she explains. In Thailand, the product will have a Stila cartoon with an elephant. In Asia, whitening creams sell very well. A whitening cream lightens the color of your skin gradually and softens your face color. Another example is fragrance. In Asia it doesn't sell well, but in Europe "it's pretty popular except in France, since the French tend to look down on American fragrances."

"The challenge in the industry is to stay a few steps ahead," Debra says. "When Stila launched the lip glaze pens, Revlon copied, then Sephora. Pretty soon everyone had them. The mass market is a little different than Stila's competition. For mass producers, the main focus is to be out there and have good sales – but a very low cost structure. Stila sells product through the artist showing you how to put on the makeup. We use a lot of brushes to blend and create a different look and feel. Stila also relies on trainers – to teach freelance artists or account executives how to sell product."

"My job is to analyze everything by department," she explains. "I work with the controller, strategic planning, sales and marketing. We are constantly asking ourselves, 'Where the brand is going? How do we increase business?' You have to examine the financial impact of taking each direction. What is the impact of advertising? How do we measure that? Do we spend our extra budget on a freelance artist? Do our doors need more traffic or higher conversion rate? Who is our customer? Stila has a young image, but our price point remains high. Is the customer going to spend her $24 on lip gloss? How do we maintain those price points? Who is our customer? How do we keep her?"

Fashion Publishing

CHAPTER 10

Publishing vis-à-vis the fashion world typically means fashion journalism, photography, illustration and graphic design. Working at a fashion magazine or trade paper is much like working at a typical publication house. Success demands excellent written and verbal communication skills and an ability to thrive in a fast-paced, high-pressure deadline oriented environment. According to *The Guide to New Consumer Magazines*, the number of magazine launches has peaked and fallen in recent years. In 1998, over 1,000 new magazines were launched as compared to 540 new magazines during the first nine months of 2002, according to a University of Mississippi study. Matthew Rose, a staff reporter at *The Wall Street Journal*, has noted, "The recession, curiously, has helped would-be publishers by creating a large talent pool of unemployed writers and editors."

Jobs

Advertising: Manages client/agency contact and generates marketing materials for clients.

Consumer marketing/circulation: Handles direct marketing of subscriptions and sales of magazines at newsstands. Creates new offerings to the consumer via mail, TV or other avenues.

Writer: Follows fashion currents through editorial reporting.

Editor: Determines noteworthy trends that set the scene in the fashion world; responsible for content of the publication.

Editorial research assistant: Checks article facts prior to publication through interviews and research to verify accuracy.

Catalog editor: Oversees all content of the catalog including proofing, visual layout, and editing.

Photographer: Captures the latest fashion trends on film.

Art director: Orchestrates the visual images and the "look" of publications. Usually experienced in research, picture editing or assigning illustrations and can use software such as Quark, Photoshop and Illustrator.

The Scoop

Jobs in publishing are often glamorous, as they include exposure to famous people and exciting events. However, journalism jobs in fashion (and journalism jobs in general) are difficult to find and don't pay well. Another drawback: many fashion journalists are expected to be as stylish as the subjects they cover. Insiders from *Vogue* say that the magazine's employees "look like they belong in the magazine." One disgruntled source contends that the company simply hires people who have "the Vogue look." While being attractive might not be part of their job descriptions, contacts admit that there is a definite pressure to look good. This focus on appearance isn't surprising, given the fashion industry's premium on beauty.

A few of the large publishing giants include Time Inc., The Hearst Corporation, Condé Nast Publications and Fairchild Publications. See below for the affiliated magazines:

Time Inc.: *InStyle, Entertainment Weekly, and People*

The Hearst Corporation: *Cosmopolitan, Esquire, Harper's Bazaar, Marie Claire, and Town & Country*

Condé Nast: *Vogue, Glamour, GQ, Allure, Lucky, and Vanity Fair*

Fairchild Publications: *Jane, Details, and W.*

Candidates should have previous journalism experience, demonstrable creativity and a commitment to integrity. "Some of the characteristics that make a Fairchild editorial employee successful," says Dena Habinsky, associate director, "are an innovative approach to journalism along with the self-motivation for 'scooping' a story and a passion for covering fashion and news." A recent job posting for a "Catalogue Editor" (the firm has an Anglophile slant) at Victoria's Secret Direct (catalog and Internet retail) lists the following responsibilities and requirements:

• Proofreading/editing all printed media in order to detect and mark for correction any grammatical, mathematical, typographical or compositional errors, adhering to formatting standards.

• Review proofed jobs to assistant catalogue coordinator.

• Provide assistant catalogue coordinator with suggested editing revisions. Refers to applicable manuals, document authors and experienced coordinators to resolve specific formatting/grammatical issues.

- Responsible for volume on an annual basis equal to 52 unique direct mail catalogues; all marketing support pieces; over 6,000 pages on an annual basis.

- Must have a minimum of 7 years experience as a professional proofreader, proven ability to proofread high volumes under extremely tight deadlines with 100% accuracy and a BA in English.

Getting Hired

According to Sally Lourenco, a writer for *Elle Girl*, "getting into publishing is not as difficult as staying in publishing." Many entry-level employees in this field have English, journalism, or comparable degrees from top schools. If you are interested in fashion editing or the visual aspects of publishing, then art and graphics classes are imperative as well as a background in fashion history. Virtually any entry-level job at a fashion magazine – from spellchecker to editorial assistant to administrative assistant – requires previous experience and/or industry connections. Summer internships at magazines qualify as experience, even if interns only staple, fax and deliver coffee; publishers value office experience. Interns should keep in touch with their supervisors after their internships have ended, as these professional relationships come in handy for the job hunt and recommendation letters. Unfortunately, many college internships are unpaid, or else, often low wages. Financial planning is a must.

Check http://asme.magazine.org/asme_internships/2002_application.pdf for internships sponsored by the American Society of Magazine Editors (ASME), the professional organization for senior editors of magazines.

At the Oxford Media and Business School (www.oxfordbusiness.co.uk), there is a nine-month Fashion Publishing Programme offered twice a year in September and January. The Fashion Publishing Program is builds an understanding of the various components of a successful fashion/lifestyle magazine, and covers not only fashion editorial content but also business strategy and key revenue sources. Most important of all, the program will give you a working knowledge of how a fashion magazine is physically laid out and produced.

When applying for any magazine position, it is crucial to study the publication. What demographic group does the magazine target? What kind of advertisements does it use? Does the magazine deal with crucial social issues or glossy beauty trends? Is the writing light, scathing, upbeat, progressive, conservative or rebellious? How much photography does the

Visit Vault at **www.vault.com** for insider company profiles, expert advice,
career message boards, expert resume reviews, the Vault Job Board and more.

V/\ULT CAREER LIBRARY   **61**

magazine use? Is it top-heavy with illustrations and graphic design? Perhaps most importantly, does this magazine mesh with your own style and sensibilities? Before you apply, you must first consider these questions. Your answers will help shape a stronger and more dynamic cover letter. Your sample work, whether it is writing, photography or art, should be similar to the magazine's current style. Computer skills and knowledge of standard editorial processes are also paramount.

Pay and Perks

The top fashion magazines are published in New York, one of the world's most expensive cities. This fact doesn't make the next any nicer: editorial salaries at fashion magazines are notoriously meager. Most entry-level employees barely cross the $20,000 threshold, although you may earn up to $26,000 if you are an assistant to the editor-in-chief. However, magazines that have larger circulations pay a lot more than others, and since job responsibilities vary greatly with titles (i.e., an associate editor at a small magazine is not on the same level as an associate editor at a larger publication), it's difficult to determine the appropriate salary ranges. While managers, writers and editors earn more, these positions require years of previous experience and toil.

Freelancing is a good way to get experience, if not money. It's not a lucrative occupation, especially for an unknown. The standard rate at magazines is one dollar a word. Three dollars a word is considered high. What's more, don't expect the market to budge: these rates have been steady for nearly 20 years, according to a recent industry study. Whether you make a career of it or do it on a part-time basis, freelancing takes a lot of legwork – making contacts with editors, sending out queries and conducting the research and writing. There are a number of monthly reports and magazines for freelancers, and numerous books to point you in the right direction. After you hit the bookstore, try the Internet for helpful freelancer advice. Try the Writer's Resource Center, at poewar.com and The Writers Markets Report, at writersmarkets.com. Mediabistro.com is a great web site for freelance jobs as well.

Vault Profile: Sally Lourenco

Fashion Editor, *Elle Girl*

Sally Lourenco has been a fashion editor for over five years. She began working at *German Vogue* for a short time as a freelance editorial assistant and gained additional experience at other publications such as Condé Nast's *Women's Sports & Fitness*, *In Style*, and *Italian Vogue*. She currently writes for *French Vogue* online and now works as a senior editor for *Elle Girl*. Sally's main goal was always to further her interest in writing while still satisfying the visual aspect of creativity. Ms. Lourenco says, "It's been a well-rounded five years, allowing me to gain knowledge of the business of publishing – especially for women's consumer publications – and the innovative thinking that keeps certain magazines at the forefront."

Apparently, the one thing that is constant in publishing is change. It can be the invariable changes of job titles, editors and positions on mastheads, or fashion's changes in styles and trends. There has been a push toward more celebrity content, such as *In Style* magazine, which combines the focus of magazines like *People* with fashion. These days, every women's consumer magazine has a few pages dedicated to celebrities – what they are wearing; how to wear what they are wearing; or where to buy what they are wearing.

Sally believes this trend ties into an increased focus on shopping. A few studies and marketing reports have tracked a decrease in the amount of time spent reading. As a result, magazines have decreased the length of features and increased the number of images and product (i.e. fashion). People seem to be relying more on magazines to shop; therefore, magazine pages have become like catalogues where editors define trends and provide options to find these trends. Features, on the other hand, follow the tabloid phenomenon with shocking headlines meant to grab the readers' attention. Sally relates, "I think during our most prosperous Internet years, the shopping, celebrity and luxury focus was at its peak. Now, people turn to more stable and fulfilling themes, so there is more international awareness and focus on the enduring aspects of fashion and enjoying life than before. Magazines are keeping the celebrity angle, since it seems to be a constant source of amusement for people."

Sally advises, "A career in publishing is an excellent place to be if you are a creative person with a bit of business sense and an eye for the zeitgeist. For people who love change and crave a fast-paced lifestyle,

Visit Vault at **www.vault.com** for insider company profiles, expert advice, career message boards, expert resume reviews, the Vault Job Board and more.

VAULT CAREER LIBRARY

63

this is the perfect industry." However, people who seek stability won't be happy. The nature of the industry changes with the focus of the reader and is greatly affected by the highs and lows of the economy. "An editor is only as good as her last idea and must also be constantly expanding their knowledge and creativity. It is precarious but also extremely fulfilling in many ways," explains Sally.

Becoming a Fashion Magazine Assistant

by Sally Melanie Lourenco

Every magazine has a different number of people on staff. Some features-focused magazines (like *Vanity Fair* and *Condé Nast Traveler*) have mostly copy, features and research editors; fashion publications have large fashion, photo and art departments; and so on. What follows is a general list of entry level editorial, fashion and art department positions, plus the scoop on getting promoted to the next level.

An introduction to the editorial assistantship

An unspoken rule here is that the level at which you assist has a great bearing on how far you will go and how quickly you will get there. Assisting lower level associate editors, some of whom have just been promoted and given their first-ever assistant, may include more menial tasks and doesn't allow for the direct experience you'd get assisting someone at the executive level.

With most assistant-level positions, salaries are usually in the same low range. Executive assistants (usually for an editor-in-chief, who has both editorial and executive assistants), however, get paid almost as much as the assistant editors, in some cases more. But you aren't in it for the money, remember?

Generally, you could be an assistant for anywhere from one to five years before you are promoted from within. It all depends on how much you learn, how fast you master your menial tasks and what kind of changes may be happening within the magazine. If you are given extra editorial writing and editing responsibilities, or if you work for an Executive Editor or Director for 1-2 years, you may be able to score an Assistant Editor's post by moving to another magazine.

The department you choose to work in will have direct bearing on how you move within the magazine. Switching directions just wastes time, so choose wisely. Select something you have a personal interest in and can dedicate yourself to for the long term.

Responsibilities

You will do grunt work and love it. Filing, opening and sorting mail, faxing, scheduling, expense reports, typing, research, making appointments, copying and anything else that will make the editors' lives easier. You'll need excellent organizational and phone skills, and be responsible for maintaining updated contact lists, juggling the phone,

Visit Vault at **www.vault.com** for insider company profiles, expert advice, career message boards, expert resume reviews, the Vault Job Board and more.

V∧ULT CAREER LIBRARY   **65**

faxing and figuring out which tasks are most important and which you can hold off on in an emergency. When you get promoted to a higher position, your success will depend on just how organized you are and how successful you've been in these areas.

This phase seems never-ending at times, but it prepares you for the mania to come. You definitely need to know Excel, Word and all Microsoft Office suite programs thoroughly. It's a plus if you are familiar with Desktop Publishing software like Quark. You'll also need to know how to draft letters, make charts and so forth. Even though you may think that personal requests such as dry cleaning, shopping and dinner reservations are not part of your job responsibility, you'll need to realize that attitude is everything. How badly do you want to make your boss' life easier, and how much will you appreciate it when someone does it for you later on?

Salaries start at $23,000 per year plus benefits, and most large magazines pay overtime. There will be a great deal of overtime, so most months it will feel like you're making $30,000 or more.

By job

Editorial assistant

Support one or more editors with daily administrative work. After all that is done, depending on what level editor you work for, you may also: keep contacts with freelance editors; preview and open manuscripts and story proposals; answer reader mail; contribute small 100- to 200-word articles to the magazine; research for feature stories; write headlines and decks; and keep track of story ideas and editorial planning.

Getting Hired

Experience at a school newspaper, magazine or freelance contributions to other smaller local publications are a plus. A journalism and/or English education is also attractive. Also consider the topics covered at the magazine of your choice – news, economics, psychology, fashion etc. Any education or background that could help you come up with relevant topics and ideas is essential. This may even help you specialize in a section such as interior design or business news.

Getting Promoted

If you handle your administrative duties well and balance any writing or editing assignments, you could be promoted to Assistant Editor level in a year. It also depends on whom you work for. If it is an executive-level editor who allows you to take on larger responsibilities, the experience will be invaluable and essential to your promotion within or at another magazine.

Fashion assistant

Responsibilities

Fashion editors and writers conceive and compose stories. For an assistant, duties include administrative work as mentioned, but may include some editing, proofreading, research, caption and headline writing. You may also be able to write small stories and reporting for the Front of Book (all the pages that come before the main feature stories and photo shoots in the middle to back of book. The Front of Book (FOB) usually contains short report-style stories).

Getting Hired

The requirements here are much the same as an editorial assistant. A genuine interest in the magazine you are working for and knowledge of the reader is essential as well. Some editors may ask you to make a list of ideas you'd have for certain FOB sections, just to see how you think. But the main concern is whether or not you will be patient enough to put in the time, do the administrative work and learn slowly. There may also be times when you are called upon to write a larger story, so any clips you have from school publications, or writing samples from essays and reports you've written, would be helpful. An internship is also a plus, as is knowledge of fashion history.

Getting Promoted

Some assistants wait two years, just to be passed over for a position for someone from the outside. Be sure to ask what your prospective employer's policy is on promoting from within. Others are gradually given more reports to write and pages to edit. It all depends on how quickly you work and how well you handle each responsibility, as well as how willing you are to learn the craft. The concern here is not to move up in title, but to accumulate clips and bylines. If you are an assistant who is allowed to write in every issue and consistently given larger assignments, it is beneficial for you to remain where you are until the right opportunity arrives.

Visit Vault at **www.vault.com** for insider company profiles, expert advice, career message boards, expert resume reviews, the Vault Job Board and more.

VAULT CAREER LIBRARY   67

Fashion market editor's assistant

There are also fashion market editors' assistants. Here you'll be doing all of the administrative work, including: calling in all the clothes for your editor's markets and assigned shoots (sometimes that means five or six shoots at once), returning all the clothes, keeping track of the items needed and similar tasks. There is a tremendous amount of follow-through involved, so you have to be meticulous. Most of your time will be spent sitting at your desk and returning clothes or accessories from the fashion closet, which means long hours. You will not be going on any appointments unless you have built a solid relationship with your editor and she is willing to let you cover some smaller markets (like sunglasses or lingerie). This usually happens after one year. There will be long hours and tremendous amounts of scheduling. If you love clothes and want to be a market editor, this is the job for you.

Getting Hired

Market editors look for people who are interested in becoming market editors. Previous work as an executive assistant in fashion will get you in, as will an internship at a major magazine working in the fashion market department. Be professional and polished in attitude and appearance. Market editors are representatives for their magazines and always look the part. A fashion education is not essential. Organization, computer skills and ability to juggle tasks are a plus.

Getting Promoted

I have seen countless assistants become frustrated with the grunt work and long hours associated with this position. Many have left and have been promoted at other types of magazines earlier than they would have been had they stayed in fashion. At fashion magazines, it is all about your boss' attitude and trust. You may start off with small markets like swimwear and lingerie or sunglasses – how well you handle these responsibilities will determine how long it will take to climb. It is a very competitive field. It's always wise to ask up front what the chances are for increased responsibilities.

Stylist's assistant

If you work for a fashion editor who styles shoots, you will be making travel arrangements, packing trunks of clothes, hauling them everywhere you go and keeping track of every last item you take with you. You will also be responsible for returning the items, calling the designers to get items in (although sometimes this is up to the market editors) and keeping track of ideas and idea boards. You'll also be going on every shoot with the editor. Warning: This is very exciting and attractive to many young aspiring editors because of the glamorous veneer, but it wears off very quickly. Unless you have a genuine interest in photography, models and the visual aspect of the craft, this is not a wise choice. You will be working every day of the week (weekends too), traveling at a moment's notice, waking up at 5 a.m. and going to bed after midnight at times. You have to love it, and realize that you are an assistant – and that most assistants suffer through similar grueling schedules and menial tasks. If you have a large ego and aren't willing to do anything and everything your editor tells you, then you should reconsider pursuing this position.

Getting Hired

Stylists look for proficient, humble, hard-working assistants. You'll be keeping longer hours then they do, and they work long hours, so you need to be dedicated. You will also be working with difficult, cranky photographers and models with major egos at times. To succeed, you must have a calm, patient and diplomatic manner, no matter what is going on around you. It is also common for stylists to request assistants that can commit to the job for more than a year, usually two to three years. Your background should include some work with photographers (perhaps assisting) or with another stylist. Fashion design and photography education are most desirable.

Getting Promoted

After two to three years working with a top-notch stylist at a major fashion publication or a cutting edge magazine, you can go to a smaller publication and style your own shoots. Most assistants begin to freelance on the side for lesser-known publications in order to build a portfolio. Without a portfolio it will take you longer. Be advised that this is tricky – most major companies do not allow employees to freelance (there may be an intellectual property clause in your contract). You could also look for an opportunity to style smaller shoots for your employer – perhaps still life styling. If you have the right eye for your magazine, you may be promoted.

Photo assistant

Administrative responsibilities abound here as well. You'll log in and return film and portfolios, correspond with photographers, assist with travel arrangements for shoots, order prints, prepare expense reports,

Visit Vault at **www.vault.com** for insider company profiles, expert advice, career message boards, expert resume reviews, the Vault Job Board and more.

VAULT CAREER LIBRARY   69

invoices and budgets, send issues to contributing photographers and organize countless files for the department.

Getting Hired

An interest in photography, especially the type used in the magazine you've chosen, is a must. Knowledge of and an educational background in photography are also beneficial. Being good with numbers and budgets is essential, as are follow-through skills. You may also have to be diplomatic when faced with irate requests from photographers and other editors.

Getting Promoted

After one year you should be able to move up to assistant or associate level, where you'll have direct relationships with photographers, organize shoots and have developed a good eye for the kind of look your magazine prefers. This takes time, however, and it all depends on how quickly you learn your craft.

Art assistant

You'll probably be doing more administrative follow-up and page proof trafficking here than anything else. There will also be photo research and art research, where you will find pictures and photographs from agencies for relevant pages. Computer proficiency is essential, since you will be using scanners, Quark and Photoshop.

Getting Hired

A BFA and folio of past layouts or design projects you've worked on in school is needed, in addition to extensive knowledge of desktop publishing programs.

Getting Promoted

To get promoted, you will have to master the look of the magazine you work for, and work under someone who allows you added responsibilities with pages. This usually comes after two years. It is an enormous responsibility to manage the total look of a magazine and many places require you to have added education in mastering copy fitting as well as visuals.

Production assistant

You'll be responsible for maintaining the deadline schedules of the magazine and following up on all internal delays, in addition to the typical administrative duties. This department focuses on all stages of editorial production, from beginning concepts, page counts and budgets to final approvals by editors and editors-in-chief. Your job will be to learn this and master it, taking some of the pressure off your supervisor.

Getting Hired

A genuine interest in management and production is essential. Don't take this job as a back door to another department. You have to be extremely organized, willing to work long hours and able to work well under pressure and when things go wrong. Knowledge of Quark and Photoshop is also a plus.

Getting Promoted

After a solid year at this job, you may be able to demonstrate the responsibility and attention to warrant a promotion. It really depends on how much your supervisor thinks you're capable of.

Copy assistant

Responsibilities

In addition to administrative duties, usually for the department and copy chief, you will be responsible for maintaining records of what pages and projects have gone through the departments as part of the production process. You may be asked to line edit short copy and fact-check on credits as well.

Getting Hired

An interest in the written word, familiarity with the *Chicago Manual of Style* and/or *AP Style Manual* and a journalism or English background is key. Experience at a newspaper or internship is also a plus. Attention to detail and the ability to work long hours under deadline to get the job done are required.

Getting Promoted

Pitching in to lighten the load wherever you can here is the fastest way to a promotion; familiarity with your magazine's writing style and effective line editing will also give you a leg up in a year.

Research Assistant

Responsibilities

This is also called fact checking. You'll be responsible for the department's administrative duties as well as any research requests that come in from other editors. This department's responsibility is to be

Visit Vault at www.vault.com for insider company profiles, expert advice, career message boards, expert resume reviews, the Vault Job Board and more.

VAULT CAREER LIBRARY

71

certain that every fact published is correct. Your job will be to help them do that. This is great for someone who loves research and fact-finding.

Getting Hired

This is also not a backdoor position into another department and there is careful screening for that. A two-year commitment is usually preferred. Attention to detail and a great deal of follow-through are essential. Also have knowledge of Lexis-Nexis, Baseline and other research sources.

Getting Promoted

Being dedicated to tackling anything, from the longest features to the smallest reports, will help you rise quickly. Promotion is more an issue of being in the right place at the right time – i.e., whenever an opening comes up.

Modeling

CHAPTER 11

A model is a person employed to display merchandise, such as clothing or cosmetics through a variety of media. In keeping with society's somewhat narrow concept of beauty, most female runway models are extraordinarily tall and thin. This gaunt ideal no doubt sends a troubling message to the vast majority of women, who are not 5'11 and 105 pounds. It also poses health risks for the models themselves due to strict dieting, especially if candidates aren't naturally lanky. The male side of modeling is no less rigorous: the most successful male models are often thin or extremely muscular. Female models typically earn more than male models for similar work. Modeling opportunities do exist for people of other sizes and shapes. These jobs often aren't as prestigious or well paying, but insiders report that they are fairly lucrative. There are also specialty-modeling jobs such as body doubling for actors and "hand modeling" for jewelry.

Jobs

Agent: Markets and manages talent. Negotiates contracts and jobs for models.

Fit model: Serves as a live person with real contours and a shape for manufacturers and fashion houses. Fit models must be the "average" size and maintain certain measurements.

Print model: Appears in catalogs, magazines, or anything that appears two-dimensional. Print models usually represent the average or most common size for that category. For example, there are petite models, large-size models, girls' models and regular fit models.

Runway model: Takes it to the catwalk and adds a third dimension to designers' creations.

Specialty model: Recruited for particular body parts such as long fingers and well-manicured nails. For example, women with well-proportioned feet are needed for shoe advertisements. Advertisements of stockings, pantyhose and razors require women with nicely shaped legs.

Visit Vault at **www.vault.com** for insider company profiles, expert advice, career message boards, expert resume reviews, the Vault Job Board and more.

VAULT CAREER LIBRARY   73

The Scoop

The first step to becoming a model is to visit a modeling agency. Insiders advise aspiring models to steer clear of "agencies" that are really schools offering expensive courses. Modeling schools provide training in posing, walking, make-up application and other basic tasks, but not necessarily job opportunities. Many agents actually prefer beginning models with little or no previous experience and discourage models from attending modeling schools and purchasing professional photographs. Agency selection is an important factor for advancement in the industry because the better the reputation of the agency, the more assignments usually available to the model. However, competition is extremely fierce at the top agencies.

A reputable agency, one insider notes, will train you for free since they only stand to benefit if you really have what it takes. A good strategy in modeling is to interview at a big agency because you will likely receive a very honest assessment of your potential. Before you approach an agency, you should have head shots, profile views, full length and ¾ length shots. If an agency is interested, they will arrange for a more extensive photo test. Once models begin building their "books," they often use several different photographers to capture a wide range of looks because it is critical to have an excellent portfolio. A portfolio is a collection of the model's previous work that is carried to all interviews and bookings. A composite card (or comp card) contains the best photographs from a model's portfolio along with his or her measurements.

Models must gather information before a job. For example, they should learn the pay, date, time, and length of the shoot from the agent. In addition, models must know if hair, make-up, and clothing stylists will be provided. It is helpful to know what product is being promoted and what image they should project. Models use a document called a "voucher" to record the rate of pay and the actual duration of the job. The voucher is used for billing purposes after both the client and model sign it. Once a job is completed, the cycle begins again as models check with their agent and look for the next booking.

Almost all models work through agents. Agents are the link between models and clients. An agency usually receives 25 to 30 percent of the model's earnings in return for the agency's services. This fee is often negotiated with top models, but inexperienced models do not have any leverage so they are charged higher commission fees. Agents also may have different fees depending on the type of job. A one-time job will carry a higher percentage fee than a yearlong contract with Calvin Klein. Agents scout for new faces, advise and train new models and promote them to clients. A typical modeling job lasts only one day, so modeling agencies differ from other employment agencies by maintaining an ongoing relationship with the model. Agents find and maintain relationships with clients, arrange auditions called "go-sees" and book shoots if a model is hired. They also provide bookkeeping and billing services and may even offer financial planning services. Because models are self-employed, they must provide their own health/retirement benefits as well as maintain detailed records of income and tax-deductible expenses. Models may have to set themselves up as their own company – and pay income taxes on a quarterly basis.

Getting Hired

Modeling jobs are concentrated in New York, Los Angeles, and Miami. One study cites that the Big Apple is home to almost 7,500 models. Fortunately for all these models, New York City, along with Paris and Milan, hosts the most fashion shows worldwide. The most difficult areas for models to crack are high fashion and runway. High fashion means "supermodel" – think Naomi Campbell, Claudia Schiffer, Cindy Crawford and Calvin Klein's favorite, Kate Moss. Only a lucky few climb to the top. One insider asserts, "The one-in-a-million chance of achieving supermodel model fame is perhaps symbolic of the whole fashion industry: many survive, but precious few thrive." Fortunately for the vast majority of aspiring models, there are a number of other areas to consider, including editorial print modeling, catalog work and commercial jobs (product advertising and billboards).

Pay and Perks

Models can earn staggering amounts of money, especially at top modeling agencies such as Ford and Elite. Insiders also report "splendid perks" such as fun, free time and fame. "Since modeling has a lot of seasonal work," comments one source, "you model when the lines are just coming out. There's lots of time in between." The same contact goes on to rave about the "fun, crazy lifestyle" and "the fun, crazy people," but only if "you're into that sort of thing."

Even catalog and hand/foot models can earn upwards of $100,000 in a year if they work regularly. Models also routinely have access to clubs and private parties and are often given clothing as a perk.

Visit Vault at **www.vault.com** for insider company profiles, expert advice, career message boards, expert resume reviews, the Vault Job Board and more.

V∧ULT CAREER LIBRARY   **75**

Vault Profile: Danita Summers

Model

Danita Summers began modeling during high school. She and her girlfriend visited an agency in San Francisco, and she signed up for her first job over the summer. One of the first things she did was a department store advertisement for "Back to School." During college, she modeled part-time to put herself through school. Danita did a lot of catalogs, print ads and even a few commercials for companies like Espirit, Sears, Robinson's May, and J.C. Penney's. Most pictures she did fell into the juniors or bridal category.

National catalogs such as J.C. Penney's paid the most – due to its national circulation and year long publication. In addition, fewer models were used than in a regular shoot, so the selected models got paid more. Print ads, the weekly inserts in the newspaper from department stores, were more work because a whole season of ads would be shot in two months or less. The potential for good pay was there but you had to work continuously. For example, says Danita, "You would start shooting in September to work on Christmas and after-Christmas advertisements. When that project ended in November, you would start shooting Spring. You have to do each rotation to continue the salary. Your agent will negotiate the price based on frequency of printing and number of copies each time. For commercials, the pay was based on national versus local reach. If the commercial was rerun years later, the company would pay you again for its use."

In college, Danita lived in St. Louis, Missouri so the work was a little different than San Francisco. Her jobs would take her to Chicago, Texas and parts of the Midwest. She was also naturally thin, which was fine for San Francisco but put her at a distinct disadvantage in the Midwest. She ended up modeling for a lot of junior clothing and Bridal catalogs and accessories. In bridal, most companies hire one model that does everything for them for a whole season. Danita explains, "You end up traveling a lot to many bridal conventions. You do find new friends when you travel, but it can get extremely tiring." She continues: "The best perk in modeling is definitely the clothes. If they alter clothes, they will give you the clothing or shoes. Typically, buyers and advertisers are really good about giving you free merchandise." The worst part of the job, she says, is "all the waiting. There are a lot of times you sit there and do nothing. Once your hair and makeup is ready, you wait for the photographer, set or whatever."

She continues, "You might try to study to pass the time, but you can't concentrate easily in a wedding dress and veil. Also, no one in modeling is that nice. After I passed the 22-year-old mark, the other models I met were only getting younger. It wasn't as fun then because most people I met were 15 to 18 years old, and it was more difficult to relate to them. There is not as much room for you to grow as other careers." Danita never pursued modeling as a career full-time, but her friends that actively pursued it did well. She estimates that if she had done a job every month, her earnings would have been $150,000 to $200,000 a year. If she had worked all the time, Danita's earnings would have topped $250,000.

Visit Vault at **www.vault.com** for insider company profiles, expert advice, career message boards, expert resume reviews, the Vault Job Board and more.

VAULT CAREER LIBRARY   77

Losing sleep over your job search?
Endlessly revising your resume?
Facing a work-related dilemma?

Super-charge your career with Vault's newest career tools: Resume Reviews, Resume Writing and Career Coaching.

Vault Resume Writing

On average, a hiring manager weeds through 120 resumes for a single job opening. Let our experts write your resume from scratch to make sure it stands out.

- Start with an e-mailed history and 1- to 2-hour phone discussion

- Vault experts will create a first draft

- After feedback and discussion, Vault experts will deliver a final draft, ready for submission

Vault Resume Review

- Submit your resume online

- Receive an in-depth e-mailed critique with suggestions on revisions within TWO BUSINESS DAYS

Vault Career Coach

Whether you are facing a major career change or dealing with a workplace dilemma, our experts can help you make the most educated decision via telephone counseling sessions.

- Sessions are 45-minutes over the telephone

"I have rewritten this resume 12 times and in one review you got to the essence of what I wanted to say!"

– *S.G. Atlanta, GA*

"It was well worth the price! I have been struggling with this for weeks and in 48 hours you had given me the answers! I now know what I need to change."

– *T.H. Pasadena, CA*

"I found the coaching so helpful I made three appointments!"

– *S.B. New York, NY*

For more information go to
www.vault.com/careercoach

VAULT
> the insider career network™

Post-MBA Options

CHAPTER 12

The Scoop

Like the entertainment industry, the fashion industry considers education to be less important than experience. So, if you want to go into the industry but don't have the previous experience, get a part-time job in sales or merchandising for an introduction to the industry. Unfortunately, most companies won't care much about your MBA unless they are large corporations, such as Gap, Levi Strauss, Eddie Bauer, Limited or Nike. These companies tend to hire for finance, supply chain issues or CRM. Typically, you need a consulting, finance or marketing background to get a post-MBA job in the industry. Very few apparel companies have established programs to specifically hire MBAs. A few companies that do hire MBAs for the more creative positions include Cartier, LVMH, Federated and the Gap.

Hillary Shor recruits for the Strategy & Business Development and Consulting and Assurance Services groups of Gap, Inc. These groups are relatively small (about 20 to 30 people per group). Almost all candidates have an MBA, although many are not hired directly as MBA graduates. Hillary says, "We actually look at what a candidate did prior to business school. The Strategy and Consulting groups look for candidates with consulting or industry experience (such as consumer products, goods or retail). Some of our candidates come from consulting firms such as A.T. Kearney and McKinsey."

The Strategy & Business Development group at Gap identifies, develops and drives longer-term strategies and initiatives that will result in profitable growth (usually with a focus on new opportunities). "Strategy involves brand management, research, as well as planning," says Hillary. Consulting and Assurance Services involves financial/operational analysis, process analysis and design and project management. Basically, this group acts as an internal consulting group for Gap. They may work with outside consultants and vendors.

Getting Hired

Build your resume correctly and you can get the interviews you need. In apparel, most of the job functions are very specific, such as design, merchandising, marketing, production and so on. Because many of the companies are small, there aren't very many traditional MBA "management"

Visit Vault at **www.vault.com** for insider company profiles, expert advice, career message boards, expert resume reviews, the Vault Job Board and more.

VAULT CAREER LIBRARY   **79**

positions. Many of the people who work at these companies may have gone to trade schools or been in the industry for a long time. For example, the president of Gucci used to work as vice president at Richard Tyler. He was young when he left Richard Tyler for Gucci, but he had started working there when he was 18.

The Gap, Limited, and Eddie Bauer all have internal consulting groups that traditionally hire MBAs. If you are interviewing for an internal consulting position, more than likely it will resemble a traditional consulting interview. You may be given a case study as part of the interview. (See the *Vault Guide to the Case Interview* for more information on this type of business interview.) Other jobs at fashion companies for MBA graduates may include planning, finance, or strategy.

Pay and Perks

MBA jobs in the fashion industry will not pay well in comparison with other MBA graduate options. Salaries may hover around the $50,000 mark. There are several options here – you work to get the experience or to learn enough to start your own business. If you are thinking of the latter, gain experience that will help you manage your own business. For example, if you want to open your own jewelry store, get a job merchandising or selling jewelry. The best way to learn all sides of the business is to experience it yourself. The pay in the fashion industry is more negotiable than other industries. Most companies will not release this information and, because these jobs are not necessarily geared toward MBAs, the salaries are not standard.

Vault Profile: Judy Chang
Fashion MBA

Judy Chang graduated from the Anderson School at UCLA with a MBA in 2002. Her previous education included a BS and Master's in industrial and operations engineering from the University of Michigan. After college, she worked as a Program Manager for DaimlerChrysler to coordinate the launch of a particular program in the automotive plants. Judy said, "I would work on program launches for each car model year and style (for specific windshield specifications). I came to Anderson knowing that I wanted to do something totally different." Judy also says, "If you really want to change careers, getting an MBA is essential. Without my MBA, I don't think I would have been able to switch careers successfully. Fashion companies would have looked at my resume and questioned my interest."

At the Anderson School, her emphasis was marketing, and it was the first time she began to seriously consider a fashion career. She had worked at Armani Exchange during college and enjoyed it – but didn't think that fashion would be a practical career choice. At Anderson, she joined the Fashion and Retail Association and began to do her research so that she could merge her interests and career goals. On campus, Macy's and Neutrogena came for interviews. Through the database, she found alumni and contacted them to speak about their experiences. Judy landed a summer internship in Planning at Macy's West. She worked there for three months in the summer and is now there full-time.

At Macy's West, Judy did two projects over the summer. (The department store Macy's is split into two regions and run completely separately. Macy's East is headquartered in NYC, while Macy's West is based in San Francisco.) To her surprise, Judy's operations experience was extremely relevant during the internship. Her first project was about handbag assortments. Her goal was to figure the optimum assortment level. Judy analyzed the number of styles bought for each cluster of stores, available table space for the handbags and discounted handbag sales versus regular stock. She used Macy's sales data as well as active visits to the Macy's floor to make her recommendations. Her second project was to standardize colors across a group of buyers. Each buyer used an individual color coding system. Macy's had no way of tracking sales by color or across categories. For example, although each buyer bought "red," each red item could be a completely different shade. Judy created a color tracking system that

Visit Vault at **www.vault.com** for insider company profiles, expert advice, career message boards, expert resume reviews, the Vault Job Board and more.

VAULT CAREER LIBRARY

81

allowed the planners to analyze the sales by color and buyer. Macy's could now see which color sold during any a one-week period.

During her internship, Judy was excited to go to work everyday (especially compared to her previous position). She found everyone to be supportive and very friendly. Macy's was a very different experience for her. Judy said, "At Macy's, it seemed like the workforce was 90 percent women and only 10 percent men. At DaimlerChrysler, I used to work with 90 percent men and 10 percent women. If there is something you really think will make you happy, you should do it – even in this difficult economy."

APPENDIX

Employer Index

Major Labels and Chain Stores

Abercrombie & Fitch
Human Resources
P.O. Box 182168
Columbus, OH 43218
(614) 283-6500
www.abercrombie.com

This venerable store and catalog merchant (an episode of M*A*S*H was based around the arrival of an Abercrombie & Fitch catalog) has focused its sales pitch on a younger crowd, age 18 through college. Applicants are welcome in corporate, full/part time store employment (the company operates its own stores with no franchising) and modeling.

The Body Shop International
New City Court
20 St. Thomas Street
London SE1 9RG
United Kingdom
0207 208 7600
http://bodyshop.e-cruitnow.com/

The Body Shop claims its first goal is "to dedicate our business to the pursuit of social and environmental change," but they certainly aren't above making money, either. The company's line of animal- and environment-friendly oils, lotions and cosmetics brought in more than $1.1 billion in 2001. Body Shop products are sold in over 1,900 locations worldwide, both in the company's own stores and in other venues.

Chanel Inc.
Human Resources
Nine West 57th Street
New York, NY 10019
(212) 303-5925
www.chanel.com

Chanel is one of the classic names in women's fashion. The private company, directed by designer Karl Lagerfeld since 1983 (Gabrielle "Coco" Chanel died in 1971), deals in ready-to-wear women's clothing, haute couture, fragrances, cosmetics, eyewear, shoes, jewelry and watches.

Dolce & Gabbana

660 Madison Avenue
New York, NY 10021
(212) 750-0055
www.dolcegabbana.it/eng/main.asp

Based in Milan, the company maintains three brands, maddeningly named "Dolce & Gabbana," "D&G" and "& Dolce&Gabbana." The latter two brands are somewhat more casual in nature, but all three provide fashions and accessories for men and women.

Eddie Bauer

P.O. Box 97000
Redmond, WA 98073-9700
(800) 625-7935
www.eddiebauer.com

Part of the Spiegel Group of companies (including Spiegel Catalog jewelry and Newport News fashions), Eddie Bauer is headquartered in the shadow of Microsoft in Redmond, Wash. The company produces sharp casual fashions for men and women, as well as accessories, home furnishings and more.

The Estée Lauder Companies Inc.

Human Resources Department
767 Fifth Avenue
New York, NY 10153
(212) 572-4200
www.elcompanies.com

The Estée Lauder Companies sell skin care, makeup, fragrance and hair care products around the world, though 60 percent of sales come from North America. The company's name brand is joined by such favorites as Aramis, Aveda and Clinique, and is the fragrance licensee for Donna Karan, Tommy Hilfiger and Kate Spade. Always popular, Estée Lauder claims 45 consecutive years of increased sales.

Gap Inc.

Two Folsom Street
San Francisco, CA 94105
(800) GAP-NEWS
www.gap.com

Gap is a triple threat in the retail business, encompassing Banana Republic and Old Navy in addition to its eponymous stores. Each has its own similar fashions as well as those of outside designers. Jobs in design, distribution, retail, corporate and internships are available through the company's main web site or through the branches.

Giorgio Armani

114 Fifth Ave., 17th Fl.
New York, NY 10011
(212) 366-9720
www.giorgioarmani.com

Known for business wear as well as high fashion, Armani licenses its name for eyewear (through its subsidiary Luxottica), cosmetics, perfumes, jeans, watches and more. The company has stores in 30 countries, where apparel makes up more than half of sales.

Gucci

Human Resources Department
Via Don Lorenzo Perosi
6 Casellina di Scandicci
Florence 50018
Italy
www.guccigroup.com

Gucci, a well-known design house and parent of design houses, provides leather goods (handbags and other leathers make up about 50 percent of sales), cosmetics, accessories and of course clothing for men and women. Companies under the Gucci umbrella include Yves Saint Laurent, Fendi, Van Cleef & Arpels, Oscar de la Renta, Balenciaga, Luxury Timepieces International and Ermenegildo Zegna. Headquarters are in Amsterdam.

Guess? Inc.

Recruiting Department
1444 South Alameda Street
Los Angeles, CA 90021
www.guess.com/guessinc.asp

Visit Vault at **www.vault.com** for insider company profiles, expert advice, career message boards, expert resume reviews, the Vault Job Board and more.

VAULT CAREER LIBRARY   87

Founded by the four Marciano brothers in 1982, Guess has grown from $8 million in sales to over $677 million in 2001. The popular brand started with jeans for men and women (at least the tall, skinny ones), but now includes a full range of apparel and and accessories for humans of all ages and most body types. Guess stores are responsible for their own recruiting, but the corporation itself hires designers, merchandisers, buyers and just about everybody else a fashion company needs to operate.

J.Crew

Human Resources
770 Broadway
New York, NY 10003
(866) CREW-TEAM
www.jcrew.com

Launched in 1983 as a catalog-only retailer, J.Crew first hit the bricks and mortar in New York's South Street Seaport in 1989. J.Crew stores, with their popular brand of casual wear for men and women, are in many locations, and the company has expanded into Web retail.

Laura Ashley Ltd.

27 Bagleys Lane, Fulham
London SW6 2QA
United Kingdom
44-20-7880-5100
www.lauraashley.com

Laura Ashley caught a lucky break in 1953, starting out selling headscarves just when Audrey Hepburn made them fashionable. Today, the British company makes fashions for women and children, home furnishings and even has a florist service.

Limited Brands Inc.

HR Direct – Résumés
P.O. Box 182414
Columbus, OH 43218-2414
careers.limitedbrands.com

With such a diverse offering of brands (The Limited, Victoria's Secret, Bath & Body Works, Structure, Lerner and others), one could argue that the company's name is misleading. Just about every option in fashion retail is available through Limited, from design and sourcing to marketing and store operations, with everything in between.

L'Oreal

575 Fifth Ave.
New York, NY 10017
(212) 818-1500
www.loreal.com

L'Oreal is a powerhouse in the skin and hair care and cosmetics industries, with brands such as Lancome, Maybelline, Matrix and Helena Rubinstein, not to mention L'Oreal. The French company is also licensed to produce fragrances under the Ralph Lauren and Giorgio Armani labels. More than 30 percent of worldwide sales come from the North America region.

Louis Vuitton

Attn: Human Resources Louis Vuitton
19 E. 57th St., 12th Fl.
New York, NY 10022
(866) 884-8866 (VUITTON)
www.vuitton.com

Louis Vuitton, part of the French conglomerate LVMH Group, designs and produces leather goods, shoes, ready-to-wear clothes and accessories for men and women. Vuitton has stores in 47 countries, and bought Donna Karan (the company, not the person) in November 2001. Other names under the LVMH aegis include Givenchy and Christian Dior.

OshKosh B'Gosh Inc.

Human Resources Department
P.O. Box 300
OshKosh, WI 54902-0300
(800) 558-0206, ext. 4395
(920) 231-8621 (Fax)
www.oshkoshbgosh.com

This venerable no-nonsense clothing maker has been around since 1895; still headquartered in the town whose name it bears, OshKosh B'Gosh has flagship stores in New York, London and Paris. While probably best known for its sturdy baby and children's clothes, OshKosh also has a line of men's wear.

Visit Vault at **www.vault.com** for insider company profiles, expert advice, career message boards, expert resume reviews, the Vault Job Board and more.

VAULT CAREER LIBRARY   89

Pacific Sunwear

Attn: (Job Title)
P.O. Box 68042
Anaheim, CA 92817
(714) 414-4000
http://www.pacsun.com/company/careers/

It began in a Newport Beach, Calif. surf shop in 1982; now it covers more than 780 locations as well as 75 retail outlets. It's a force of nature – it's Pacific Sunwear. No longer content to deal in surfwear, swimwear and beach clothes, Pacific Sunwear deals in all casual wear for men and women, including accessories and shoes. Don't look for boardroom or night club apparel in these shops.

Polo Ralph Lauren Corporation

Human Resources Department
650 Madison Avenue
New York, NY 10022
(800) 377-7656
www.polo.com

Ralph Lauren's fashion company makes fragrances, accessories, men's/women's/kid's clothes and even home accessories (as in house wear). Polo Ralph Lauren is also active in several philanthropic ventures, including the Pink Pony Project to provide healthcare for disadvantaged children.

Reebok International Ltd.

1895 J.W. Foster Boulevard
Canton, MA 02021
(781) 401-5000
www.reebok.com

Reebok makes a broad range of athletic shoes, and owns the Rockport brand of hiking boots and dress shoes. Other interests include athletic clothing, exercise equipment and sporting accessories. The Canton, Mass. location is the world headquarters of this formerly British corporation.

Revlon Inc.

625 Madison Ave.
New York, NY 10022
(212) 527-4000
www.revlon.com

Revlon is all about cosmetics, beauty tools (tweezers and the like) and fragrances, selling its products in 100 countries. Top brands other than Revlon itself include Ultima II, Almay, Charlie, Flex, Colorsilk and Mitchum.

The Wet Seal Inc.

26972 Burbank

Foothill Ranch, California 92610

(800) 735-7325

http://wetsealinc.com/careers/careers.asp

"Style is ageless," claims the company, so the stores (Wet Seal, Contempo Casuals, Arden B. and Zutopia) cater to every fashion-conscious woman age 5 and up – really. The company has more than 480 stores, of one name or another, across the U.S. and its territories. Designers, buyers and corporate people are welcome to apply, as are store personnel.

Modeling Agencies

Boss Models

1 Gansevoort St.

New York, NY 10014

(212) 242-2444

www.bossmodels.com

Boss claims to have invented the male supermodel, a specialty reflected in the agency's stable and its contracts with Calvin Klein and Ralph Lauren. An equal opportunity employer of striking looks, Boss also has a number of women.

Elite Models

111 East 22nd Street

New York, NY 10010

(212) 529-9700

www.elitemodel.com

Elite is another of the biggest names in modeling, and has been in and out of first place in recognition. Lara Flynn Boyle, Claudia Schiffer and First Family niece/granddaughter Lauren Bush all use Elite, along with 750 other models (some of them male) on five continents. The agency also sponsors the annual Elite Model Look contest, a talent search for new faces.

Visit Vault at **www.vault.com** for insider company profiles, expert advice, career message boards, expert resume reviews, the Vault Job Board and more.

VAULT CAREER LIBRARY   91

Ford Models

142 Greene St.
New York, NY 10012
(212) 219-6500
www.fordmodels.com

Ford is among the oldest (founded in 1946) and best known modeling agencies in the world. It's also the one that made models top money-earners, starting with Lauren Hutton in 1974. Current supermodel clients include Stephanie Seymour and Tomiko. Ford also handles plus sizes, men, children, parts, print models and "classic," or older women (including 1970s sensation Twiggy).

Q Model Management

180 Varick St.
13th Floor
New York, NY 10014
(212) 807-6777
www.qmodels.com

Q is a new agency (founded in 1998) making a name for itself in New York and L.A., using the Web to handle much of its business. The site is also home to Q Interactive, the agency's newsletter/magazine. The agency holds open calls for male and female models, and encourages newcomers to the business.

Storm Model Agency

5 Jubilee Place
London SW3 3TD
United Kingdom
09068 515 255
www.stormmodels.com

Founded by Sarah Doukas and funded by Richard Branson, Storm represents some of the world's most photographed faces and bodies. Storm built its reputation on legendary supermodel Kate Moss, and also works with Elle Macpherson, Devon Aoki and a host of other boys and girls (that's what they call them).

Department Stores

Dillard's Inc.

1600 Cantrell

Little Rock, AR 72201

(501) 376-5200

www.dillards.com

Dillard's operates more than 330 department stores in 29 American states, mostly in the Southeast, South and Midwest. Together, they pull in about $8.3 billion a year catering to the apparel and home furnishing needs of Mr. and Mrs. Consumer. The company's web site provides detailed information on non-sales positions at 13 different corporate locations.

Meijer

Attn: Employment Services

2727 Walker Ave. NW

Grand Rapids, MI 49544-1369

(800) 219-9150, ext. 15250

www.meijer.com

Founded as a grocery store in 1934 by a barber on $338 worth of merchandise, Meijer now has 75 department stores in five Midwest states. The family-owned partnership keeps its stores open 24 hours a day, 364 days a year, selling everything from roast beef to microwave ovens. If putting clothes on people's backs in the heartland appeals to you, this is a company to consider.

Federated Department Stores Inc.

7 West Seventh Street

Cincinnati, OH 45202

(513) 579-7000

www.fds.com/

Who? Bloomingdale's, Macy's, Bon Marche and Burdines, that's who. With those big names and more on the menu, Federated boasts one of 100 largest workforces in the world. Interested parties may contact Federated directly or apply through an affiliated company.

Visit Vault at **www.vault.com** for insider company profiles, expert advice, career message boards, expert resume reviews, the Vault Job Board and more.

V/\ULT CAREER LIBRARY   **93**

J.C. Penney Corporation

6501 Legacy Drive
Plano, TX 75024
(972) 431-1000
https://jcpdmz1.jcpenney.com/Career_Opportunities/index.asp

Though it has been feeling the economic crunch, J.C. Penney remains a powerful and recognizable force in apparel retailing. Department stores (complete with salons), catalog sales and an online portal keep the money rolling in. Jobs in sales, management, decorating and support may be researched through Penney's career site.

Kohl's Department Stores

Attn: Human Resources
N56 W17000 Ridgewood Drive
Menomonee Falls, WI 53051
(262) 703-7000
www.kohlscorporation.com

Despite the recent hard financial times, Kohl's experienced sales increases of more than 20 percent in 2001. Aggressive growth throughout the U.S. is making this department store a serious competitor to Wal-Mart and Target.

May Department Stores Co.

611 Olive Street
St. Louis, MO   63101
www.mayco.com

May, in operation since 1877, is a $14-billion retailer with several well-known stores in its stable: Filene's, Lord & Taylor, David's Bridal and Hecht's are just a few of the 11 trade names. The company acquired Priscilla's of Boston, an upscale bridal gown retailer, in 2002. Several people at May handle human resources and college recruiting, based on type of position desired; check the web site for the appropriate contact.

The Neiman Marcus Group

One Marcus Square
1618 Main Street
Dallas, TX 75201
(214) 741-6911
www.neimanmarcuscareers.com

The Dallas, Tex.-based Neiman Marcus Group operates 35 department stores and a catalog business under its own name, as well as both Bergdorf

Goodman locations in New York. The company's list of designer brands reads like a Who's Who in fashion. This upscale retailer saw sales in Specialty Retail (the stores) decline 2.9 percent in 2002 to $2.9 billion, the first such decline in five years. The $200 urban-legend cookie recipes must not be selling well this year.

Target Corporation

1000 Nicollet Mall
Minneapolis, MN 55403
(612) 304-6073
www.target.com

Another of the mega-department store companies, Target (formerly Dayton Hudson) caters to consumers at all levels: Target stores for discount merchandise, Mervyn's for the middle income and Marshall Field's for more upscale shoppers. The company also operates clothing supply companies and catalog retailers.

Wal-Mart Stores Inc.

702 SW Eighth St.
Bentonville, AK 72716
(479) 273-4000
www.walmartstores.com

Wal-Mart is the world's biggest retailer, with over 4,600 stores and 15 percent sales growth in 2001. While the idea of "Wal-Mart fashion" may generate raised eyebrows in some snooty circles, clothing sold in these stores garbs more people than that from all the world's trendy boutiques combined.

Visit Vault at **www.vault.com** for insider company profiles, expert advice, career message boards, expert resume reviews, the Vault Job Board and more.

VAULT CAREER LIBRARY   95

Use the Internet's
MOST TARGETED
job search tools.

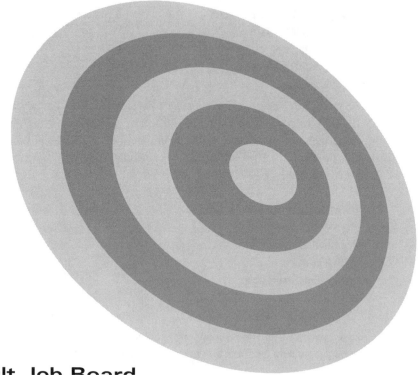

Vault Job Board

Target your search by industry, function, and experience level, and find the job openings that you want.

VaultMatch Resume Database

Vault takes match-making to the next level: post your resume and customize your search by industry, function, experience and more. We'll match job listings with your interests and criteria and e-mail them directly to your inbox.

Recommended Reading

Some of these books can be found at your local bookstore, others must be special ordered as textbooks. Quite a few may be found used at Half.com – especially those that are a few years old.

Agins, Teri. *The End of Fashion (The Mass Marketing of the Clothing Business).* ISBN: 0060958200
A Wall Street Journal writer examines the fashion industry from a business perspective.

Ash, Mary Kay. *Mary Kay You Can Have It All: Lifetime Wisdom from America's Foremost Woman Entrepreneur.* ISBN: 0761506470
Mary Kay may be the most successful woman entrepreneur in the world today, but she started her company as a single mother supporting three children – using her total life savings of $5,000. She managed to create a multibillion-dollar international company as well as a fulfilling life that reflects her values.

Barry, Mary E.; Gillespie, Karen R. and Isabel Barnum Wingate. *Know Your Merchandise: For Retailers and Consumers.* ISBN: 0070710163
Topics range from textiles, clothing, and jewelry to furniture and fine dinnerware.

Becklund, Laurie (Contributor) and J.B. Strasser. *Swoosh: The Unauthorized Story of Nike and the Men Who Played There.* ISBN: 0887306225
Entertaining and informative corporate history traces the rise, fall and recovery of Nike, the world-famous supplier of athletic shoes and casual clothing.

Bertelli, Patrizio; Rem Koolhaas (Editor), Michael Kubo, and Miuccia Prada. *Projects for Prada Part 1.* ISBN: 8887029180
Documents the collaboration between designer Miuccia Prada and Koolhaas (who designed three new "epicenter" stores for the company – in New York City, Los Angeles, and San Francisco – and created Prada's web site) that illustrates how they've rethought the shopping experience.

Bryant, Nancy O. and Leslie Davis Burns. *The Business of Fashion: Designing, Manufacturing, and Marketing.* ISBN: 1563670739
Textbook that uses actual companies for examples and at the end of each chapter. Text also includes job profiles.

Visit Vault at **www.vault.com** for insider company profiles, expert advice, career message boards, expert resume reviews, the Vault Job Board and more.

VAULT CAREER LIBRARY   97

Forden, Sara Gay. *The House of Gucci: A Sensational Story of Murder, Madness, Glamour, and Greed.* ISBN: B00006F7IW
Former Women's Wear Daily correspondent writes about Gucci, financial shenanigans and vicious family quarrels ending in a sensational murder.

Frankel, Susannah and Claire Wilcox (Preface). *Visionaries: Interviews With Fashion Designers.* ISBN: 0810965895
Collection of in-depth interviews with 23 of the world's top couturiers.

Frings, Gini Stephens. *Fashion: From Concept to Consumer (7th Edition).* ISBN: 0130335711
Textbook offers complete coverage on product processes and global influences on the evolution of the entire fashion industry.

Hagen, Kathryn. *Illustration For Designers – Second Edition.* ISBN: 0970430353

Lauder, Estee. *Estee a Success Story: A Success Story.* ISBN: 0394551915
An introduction to how Estee Lauder began her business and grew it into a cosmetics empire.

Leuzzi, Linda. *A Matter of Style : Women in the Fashion Industry (Women Then – Women Now).* ISBN: 0531158314
Explains many of the available jobs in the fashion industry.

Madsen, Axel. *Chanel: A Woman of Her Own.* ISBN: 0805016392
Coco Chanel is known for her fashion and perfume empire.

Marcus, Stanley. *Minding the Store: A Memoir.* ISBN: 1574410393
Stanley Marcus recounts the growth of his family business and the stories of customer demands and service that created a hugely profitable retail empire.

Mathiasen, Carolyn and Pamela Varley. *The Sweatshop Quandary: Corporate Responsibility on the Global Frontier.* ISBN: 1879775530
Includes information about international conventions against sweatshop labor, corporate codes of conduct and specific reports of labor conditions in several developing countries.

Matthias, Rebecca. *MothersWork.* ISBN: 0385495900
Entrepreneurial story about the apparel industry. The subtitle of the book is "How a Young Mother Started a Business on a Shoestring & Built It into a Multi-million Dollar Company."

Roddick, Anita. *Business as Unusual: The Triumph of Anita Roddick.*
ISBN: 0722539878
This company biography is a firsthand account on how to create, nurture and
run a successful company.

Peiss, Kathy. *Hope in a Jar: The Making of America's Beauty Culture.*
ISBN: 0805055517
Covers the history of the American beauty industry.

Phaidon Press (Editor). *The Fashion Book.* ISBN: 0714841188
A thorough guide with over 400 entries that includes fashion designers,
photographers, models, retailers, illustrators and icons.

Spector, Robert. *The Nordstrom Way: The Inside Story of America's # 1
Customer Service.* ISBN: 0471355941
A guide to becoming the best at customer service in any industry, using the
methods employed by the successful Seattle-based retailer.

Teicholz, Tom (Contributor) and Marvin Traub. *Like No Other Store:
The Bloomingdale's Legend and the Revolution in American Marketing.*
ISBN: 0812919637
An autobiographical account of the rise and fall of one of the nation's most
dazzling shopping emporiums, written by its former longtime chairman.

Underhill, Paco. *Why We Buy: The Science of Shopping.* ISBN:
0684849143
In an effort to determine why people buy, Paco Underhill and his detail-
oriented band of retail researchers have camped out in stores over the course
of 20 years, dedicating their lives to the "science" of shopping.

Visit Vault at **www.vault.com** for insider company profiles, expert advice,
career message boards, expert resume reviews, the Vault Job Board and more.

V/\ULT CAREER LIBRARY   **99**

Fashion Schools

Academy of Art College
San Francisco, CA

BFA and MFA programs in fashion design, textiles, knitwear, merchandising and fashion illustration.

Art Center College of Design
Pasadena, CA

BFA or BS degree in advertising, environmental design, film, fine art, graphic design, illustration, photography, product design, and transportation design. Graduate programs in fine art, design, and critical theory.

Auburn University
Auburn, Alabama

Undergraduate and graduate programs in textile engineering.

California Design College
Los Angeles, CA

Two-year AAS degrees in advanced fashion design, visual merchandising, fashion merchandising and apparel manufacturing. Certificate courses in CAD technology and fashion design.

Clemson University
Clemson, South Carolina

The School of Material Science and Engineering has various research and teaching interests, but its primary concentrations include textiles, materials science and engineering, fiber science, and polymer science.

Cornell University
Ithaca, NY

Undergraduate and graduate degrees in apparel design, apparel and textile management, and fiber science

Fashion Institute of Design & Merchandising/FIDM
Throughout CA

Offers AAS degrees and advanced study programs in fashion design, interior design, fashion merchandise marketing, textile design, visual communications, graphic design, cosmetics and fragrance merchandising, theatre costume, international manufacturing and product development and apparel manufacturing management

Visit Vault at **www.vault.com** for insider company profiles, expert advice, career message boards, expert resume reviews, the Vault Job Board and more.

VAULT CAREER LIBRARY   101

Fashion Institute of Technology
New York, NY

Provides career preparation in more than 30 fashion and design related fields, leading to Associate in Applied Science, Bachelor of Fine Arts, Bachelor of Science and Masters of Fine Arts degrees. Certificate programs also available.

Georgia Institute of Technology
Atlanta, Georgia

The School of Textile & Fiber Engineering prepares students for rewarding careers in the Polymer/Fiber/Fiber Products (PFFP) Industrial Complex. Graduates obtain positions in design, process and plant engineering, manufacturing, technical service, sales, product and process development, research, quality control and corporate management.

London College of Fashion
London, United Kingdom

Students at London College of Fashion automatically become members of the London Institute, Europe's largest center for education in art, communication, design and related technologies. The mission of the London Institute is to be at the forefront of learning, creativity and practice in arts, communication and design.

Otis College of Art and Design
Los Angeles, CA

BFA in fashion design available.

Parsons School of Design
New York, NY

Offers degree and non-degree programs in fashion design and design marketing. Locations in New York City and Paris.

Philadelphia University School of Textiles
Philadelphia

Undergrad and graduate programs in textile design, textile technology, Textile engineering, and textile materials science.

Trade Technical College

Los Angeles, CA

Offers two-year arts and science associate degrees in fashion and visual merchandising.

Texas Woman's University

Dallas, TX

Majors and minors available in fashion design, fashion merchandising, and textiles and apparel.

Visit Vault at **www.vault.com** for insider company profiles, expert advice, career message boards, expert resume reviews, the Vault Job Board and more.

VAULT CAREER LIBRARY   103

Glossary

Action plan: Buyers, merchandisers, and production people use an "action plan" or "time and action plan" to track garments in production. Usually, the plan will follow a particular order from start to end.

For example: Long sleeve shirt for delivery 9/30 to Macy's.
Fit sample approved 6/15
Fabric in house 6/30
Pieces sent out for assembly 7/15
Garments received 8/15
Garments sent out for dyeing 8/22
Garments received back for quality control inspection 9/01
Garments tagged and ready to ship out 9/15

Assortment management: Allows retailers to offer the right amount of product at the right time. Retailers accomplish this through forecasts and analysis of consumer preferences, buying patterns and buying trends.

Barcode label: A printed label containing black and white coded images meeting industry standards for routing packages or retrieving information about the box or merchandise to which the label is attached.

Category: A related assortment of items (e.g., ladies and misses clothes).

Category killer: Discount retailer that offers a complete assortment in a category and thus dominates a category from the customer's perspective.

Centralized buying: A situation in which a retailer makes all purchase decisions at one location, typically the headquarters.

Channel of distribution: Comprises all of the businesses and people involved in the physical movement and transfer of ownership of goods and services from producer to consumer.

Cooperative (co-op) advertising: Occurs when a manufacturer or wholesaler and a retailer, or two or more retailers, share advertising costs.

Customer relationship management (CRM): The automation of integrated business processes involving customers – sales (contact management, product configuration), marketing (campaign management, telemarketing) and customer service (call center, field service).

Depth of assortment: Refers to the variety in any one goods/service category with which a retailer is involved.

Electronic data interchange (EDI): The computer-to-computer exchange of business documents from retailer to vendor and back, such as purchase orders.

Fiber: Fine, flexible and threadlike filament, used to make yarns or cloth.

Fit model: Represents the firm's target customer. Compared to the runway models, fit models are usually shorter, fuller through the bust and of average proportions. The fit model is supposed to provide feedback about the garment, such as ease of movement and comfort.

Fit sample: Sample used to ensure that the garment specifications are correct before approval for mass production.

Flat sketch: Drawing of a garment that is limited to two dimensions only (front and back).

Floor-ready merchandise: Items that are received at the store in condition to be put directly on display without any preparation by retail workers.

Gross margin: The difference between the retail price the customer pays for merchandise and the cost of the merchandise (the price the retailer paid at wholesale).

Haute couture: Top designers of custom-made clothing.

Letter of credit: A letter issued by a bank authorizing the bearer to draw a stated amount of money from the issuing bank, its branches or other associated banks or agencies. Allows importers to offer secure terms to exporters.

Licensed brands: Brands for which the licensor (owner of a well-known name) enters a contractual arrangement with a licensee (a retailer or a third party). The licensee either manufactures or contracts with a manufacturer to produce the licensed product and pays a royalty to the licensor. Many fashion designers license their names, such as Ralph Lauren.

Loom: The frame or machine on which a cloth is woven.

Markdown: A reduction from selling price to meet the lower price of another retailer, adapt to inventory overstocking, clear out shopworn merchandise, reduce assortments of odds and ends or increase customer traffic.

Markup: The difference between merchandise costs and retail selling price.

Masthead: The statement of title, ownership, editors, etc., of a newspaper or periodical. In the case of newspapers, it is commonly found on the editorial page at the top of page one, and in the case of periodicals, on the contents page.

Merchandising: Consists of the activities involved in acquiring particular goods and/or services and making them available at the places, times and prices and in the quantity to enable a retailer to reach its goals.

Open to buy (OTB): The difference between planned purchases and stock already ordered.

Performance measures: The criteria used to assess retailer effectiveness. They include total sales, average sales per store, sales by goods/service category, sales per square foot, gross margins, gross margin return on investment, operating income, inventory turnover, markdown percentages, employee turnover, financial ratios and profitability.

Piece goods: Fabric that is either woven or knit.

Private-label brand: A brand of products that is produced by a store. This is also known as a store brand. The brand carries the store's own names or a name that it has created. For example, Sears has Kenmore store brand appliances and May's has Charter Club store brand clothes.

Quick response (QR): Enables a retailer to reduce the amount of inventory it keeps on hand by ordering more frequently and in lower quantities.

Reach: The number of distinct people exposed to a retailer's ads in a specified period.

Sales forecasting: Retailer estimate of expected future sales for a given time period.

Same-store sales: Sales dollars generated only by those stores that have been open more than a year and have historical data to compare this year's sales to the same time-frame last year.

Sell-through analysis: A comparison between actual and planned sales to determine whether early markdowns are required or whether more merchandise is needed to satisfy demand.

Shrinkage: The difference between the recorded value of inventory (at retail) based on merchandise bought and the retail value of actual inventory in stores and distribution centers divided by retail sales during a time period.

Visit Vault at **www.vault.com** for insider company profiles, expert advice, career message boards, expert resume reviews, the Vault Job Board and more.

VAULT CAREER LIBRARY   **107**

Shrinkage is caused by employee theft, by customer shoplifting and by merchandise being misplaced, damaged or mispriced.

Trim: Decoration or ornaments for clothing such as lace, buttons, ribbon, flowers, leather, etc.

Trunk show: A traveling collection of designer clothing or jewelry, displayed in various stores. Many designers have trunk shows to launch a new season or collection.

Universal Product Code (UPC): A classification for coding data onto products by a series of thick and thin vertical lines. It lets retailers record data instantaneously as to the model number, size, color and other factors when an item is sold, and to transmit the data to a computer monitoring unit sales, inventory levels and other factors.

Vendor: Any firm, such as a manufacturer or distributor, from which a retailer obtains merchandise.

Yarn: Fibers that are spun or twisted together.

Internet Resources

These web sites contain information about the industry, trends and jobs. Although most are free, others require subscription access.

cottoninc.com
Cotton Incorporated is a research and promotion company aiming to increase the demand for and profitability of cotton by providing value-added programs and services both in the U.S. and internationally for producers, mills, manufacturers and retailers. This site has good information about textiles.

fashioninformation.com
This subscription-based web site is a source of international apparel trends. Reports for subscribers includes updates on trends and detailed illustrations, pictures and color charts.

fashioncareercenter.com
Retail and apparel jobs are listed. The site offers other services such as resume and career advice. Employers pay membership fees to post jobs.

fashion.net/jobs
Job postings include modeling and makeup artist positions in addition to industry positions.

fashionwindows.com
This web site covers fashion trends, runway shows, fashion reviews, designers and models as well as the latest news and visuals.

global-color.com
Forecasting company that provides great information and inspiration for color in the fashion and interior design industries. Find the trends and the colors for S/S (Spring/ Summer) and A/W (Autumn/ Winter).

infomat.com
InfoMat covers the men's, women's and children's markets for apparel, textile and accessories professionals. The web site has many useful links and explanations.

jobsinfashion.com
Another job search site. Jobsinfashion.com allows you to post your resume as well.

Visit Vault at **www.vault.com** for insider company profiles, expert advice, career message boards, expert resume reviews, the Vault Job Board and more.

VAULT CAREER LIBRARY   **109**

mediabistro.com

A resource center for media professionals with job postings, resumes and discussion threads.

scott-thaler.com

This executive search and recruitment firm places professionals in the apparel, retail, beauty, luxury goods, accessories, home fashions, textile and transportation industries nationwide.

style.com

This online home of *Vogue* and *W.* magazine features complete fashion shows coverage (videos and photos), trend reports, celebrity style, expert advice and fashion news.

stylecareers.com

One of the largest fashion-only job listing web sites. Extensive job listings for apparel and textile as well as helpful links and career tips.

textilejobs.com

A simple web site that specializes in textile jobs.

wgsn.com

This subscription-based site offers fast access to all aspects of international style information. There is limited free daily news available.

woolmark.com

The Woolmark Company is a commercial organization dedicated to wool promotion. The web site also contains industry news.

About the Author

Holly Han: Holly has over nine years of experience in the apparel and textile industries. Ms. Han has developed product and designed textiles for companies such as Express, J.C. Penney and Macy's. As a consultant, she helped 7thonline.com and SmartWear define their business model and plans. At the Anderson Graduate School of Management at UCLA, Holly was the Vice President of the Management Consulting Association and received a fellowship from the Young Presidents' Organization; she also wrote a technology column for the Anderson weekly paper. Ms. Han holds degrees from the University of California at Berkeley and the Fashion Institute of Technology. She is currently Chief Operating Officer of SmartWear, a company that is developing a new class of patented smart textiles and partially funded by the National Institute of Health.

Visit Vault at **www.vault.com** for insider company profiles, expert advice, career message boards, expert resume reviews, the Vault Job Board and more.

VAULT CAREER LIBRARY   111

Use the Internet's
MOST TARGETED
job search tools.

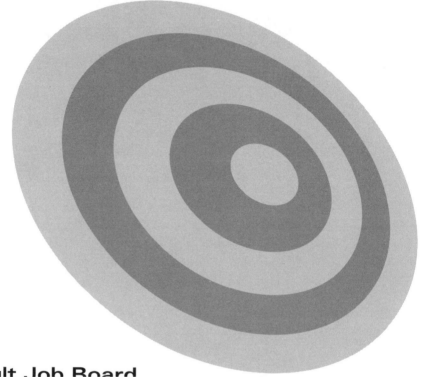

Vault Job Board

Target your search by industry, function, and experience level, and find the job openings that you want.

VaultMatch Resume Database

Vault takes match-making to the next level: post your resume and customize your search by industry, function, experience and more. We'll match job listings with your interests and criteria and e-mail them directly to your inbox.

V/\ULT
> the insider career network™